What God Can Do

Letters to My Mom from the Medical Mission Field of Togo, West Africa

By SHIRLEY CROPSEY

with Ashley C. Shannon

Cover Design by: Anna Burrous

Author photo by: Elisabeth Joy Wilson

All views are that of the author. This book is not endorsed by any of the organizations mentioned and does not necessarily represent their perspective.

Soli Deo Gloria

CONTENTS

Note from the Editor

More than ten years ago, while on a visit to my husband's extended family, my husband's aunt, Shirley Cropsey, shared her vision of one day writing a book about her experience in Togo, West Africa. She had hundreds and hundreds of letters she had written to her mom during this time in her life, and she thought the stories would make a great read.

"I'd read that book!" I said, curious to know more about my husband's extended family.

Shirley admitted that the letters had sat in her basement for a long time, and it was all a little overwhelming for her.

"Would you like me to organize them for you?" I asked. Minutes later, my husband hauled a huge box of letters to our car.

"I hope there's no African spiders in here!" I said.

"Only Michigan ones," she smiled.

The next year's visit, I handed back two large 3-ring binders of organized letters. She handed me another box full of letters. The following visit, I gave her two more binders of letters.

"Now what do I do?" she asked.

"Maybe you could start reading the letters and that will spark your ideas for the book," I suggested.

On the subsequent visit, I causally asked, "How's the book coming?"

"Not very well," she admitted.

"Would you like me to start typing out some of the letters?" I asked.

"Oh, I couldn't have you do that! You just had a baby!"

But I insisted. One step led to the next, and in between my own family's cross-country moves, another baby added to our family, and annual visits, Shirley and I worked on the text in this book.

The following pages are the result. They are Shirley's original letters to her mom, dated from 1981 to 1993. Included are personal letters and more general newsletters from the time period she and her family prepared and became medical missionaries to Togo, West Africa.

Letters were Shirley's main form of communication to all her prayer supporters and family back in Michigan. Communication via the phone was difficult and expensive.

The letters have been edited for consistency, clarity, and length. Context has been added to help readers who are unfamiliar with people, history, and locations in the Cropsey story. Because of the similarity of African names and the quickness of Shirley's cursive handwriting, some of the original names have been changed. Also, through the years of collaborative work in Togo, the Cropsey family worked with many people including Togolese nationals, fellow career missionaries, and short-term missionaries. Unfortunately, because of length, not all the people or stories she wrote about in the original letters could be included in this text.

Some newsletters, especially when Shirley was ill, were penned by Shirley's husband, Bob. These letters have been reworded to Shirley's perspective and included in the text to fill in the gaps of those time frames.

At one point, when we had been working on the project for a long time but hadn't gotten far, Shirley asked, "Will anyone want to read this?"

I felt a strong, passionate answer bubble up: *Yes.*

"Future generations of the Cropsey family will want to have a record of God's faithfulness in your life! It will be worth it," I said.

So we continued with that in mind.

Unlike the Israelite children who continually forgot God's faithfulness and turned to their own ways, Shirley and I want these letters to be a remembrance of all God has done in the Cropsey family.

I am amazed how God leads and blesses when we choose to obey His calling in our lives. Shirley's story may be very different from your own, but God has a plan for each of us that we can only accomplish through Him!

May you be encouraged by Shirley's story, and may you, in return, encourage others. It has been my pleasure to be a part of this project.

Ashley C. Shannon

Before Togo ...

Long before my family and I stepped foot in Togo, West Africa, God was preparing me for the medical mission field.

I grew up on a farm in southwest Michigan. As a child, my first introduction to Christ's love was through my parents. I was a young girl when they became Christians, and it changed everything for our family. Whenever the church doors were open, our family was there to attend. My parents were not perfect parents, but they were always striving and growing. I liked my mom's translation of the Bible best—she translated it into everyday life.

Our family verse was Romans 8:28, "And we know that God causes all things to work together for good to those who love God, to those who are called according to His purpose." As I grew, God cared for me in unique ways. He was preparing me for His work.

One day as I cleaned the house, the Holy Spirit spoke to my heart. Because I had attended church so often, I knew the Bible verse of Romans 6:23, "For the wages of sin is death, but the gracious gift of God is eternal life in Christ Jesus our Lord." I realized that my life was much like the house I was cleaning. I was basically a good person, but I needed God to deep clean my heart. The conviction was so great that I stopped cleaning and immediately prayed for God to forgive my sins.

It wasn't long after, as a new Christian and new reader, that my mom gave me the book *Ankie Comes to America* by Dena Korfker. This was my first introduction to world missions. As the years passed, the Lord used the Bible and other cultural encounters through our small church to keep my heart sensitive towards the needs of people around the world.

I attended Bible school for one year, and then in 1967, I married my childhood friend and high school sweetheart, Bob Cropsey. We were young and juggled married life with school. Both of us had been impacted by missions at a young age and knew it would be a part of our future. I graduated with a nursing degree, and while Bob attended medical school, I worked long hours as a nurse. Because of this, when Bob graduated from medical school, we were debt-free.

For six years we struggled with infertility. After fertility medications, surgery, and four miscarriages, we welcomed our first son, Luke. Soon after came our other sons: Matt, Josh, and John.

Just before Matt was born in 1974, Bob was deployed for his tour of sea duty for the Navy. He was the doctor on the ship *USS Iwo Jima*.

While I was in labor with Matt, Bob's ship collided with another ship. Fortunately, there was only minor damage and few injuries, but it meant the ship had to head to port for repairs. This gave Bob the opportunity to see baby Matt, who had a high bilirubin count at birth. I also had developed clots in my legs, and Bob was able to spend a little time with me in the hospital before he returned to his assignment.

When I was released from the hospital, my mom, who had been taking care of toddler Luke, went to the doctor for a lump that had developed under her arm. We didn't think much of it until the diagnosis came back: advanced cancer. (We didn't know it at the time, but my mom would be diagnosed and recover four times from advanced cancers.) As a new mom of two kids whose husband was away at sea, I took charge of my parents' household. Along with taking care of my mom, infant, and toddler, I watched over the baby turkeys that my parents raised because my dad was working nights at a factory. This time was stretching to my strength and energy, but God still had more lessons in store for me.

Our third son Joshua was born in 1976. One morning, Luke was playing in the basement where the free-standing fireplace stood. Luke called to me and started running toward the stairs. Immediately, I could see the flames coming across the basement ceiling. I grabbed baby Josh from his crib and called for Matt. We rushed outside, without coats, into the worst snowstorm of the season. At the neighbor's house, only a few short steps away, we called the fire department.

Before the fire department could arrive, I went back to the house to see if I could save anything but was unable to enter. The house was full of dark, billowy smoke. The fire spread quickly, and we lost everything.

We clung to the promise that "My God will supply all your needs according to His riches in glory in Christ Jesus." (Philippians 4:19) We were blown away as God provided for us, even down to the fine detail of matching crib and dresser from two different donors!

Several months before our house burned, Bob had been hospitalized. In the middle of the night, I got a call that said Bob was in the ER. Irritated, I hung up. *Of course, Bob,* who was a surgical resident at the time, *was in the ER!* It never occurred to me, until later, that they were calling to tell me that Bob had become a *patient.* When I became more alert, I called back, and indeed, Bob had been admitted into the ER after having lots of pain while operating on another patient with his attending physician. At first, the doctors thought Bob was having a heart attack.

While Bob was in the hospital, my mind raced with anxiety. I asked God, "How can I take care of three small children by myself?" But after several days and more puzzling symptoms, Bob's attending physician performed an exploratory surgery to discover a gangrenous appendix. Because of its size and position, Bob's symptoms had been atypical and a mystery. But through the situation, we were able to share our faith with Bob's boss and other employees at the hospital.

Bob had barely recovered and we were still reeling from the fire when he received a phone call from a former pastor telling us of a great need at the Christian Memorial Hospital in Bangladesh. We knew God had put medical missions on our hearts, but since Bob had missed so much time in his residency, he was hesitant to talk to his boss about taking time off for us to travel to Bangladesh. But he did, and with his boss's blessing, we were on our way to Bangladesh for a short-term trip.

Little did we know that our "yes" and a month-long stay in Bangladesh would shape so much of the next steps in our life's journey. While in Bangladesh, we were amazed at God's protection over our family. Our three boys walked down into a pit of live coals, leftover from a Christmas celebration. The heat melted the rubber from the bottom of their tennis shoes, but they came out without any burns on their feet or elsewhere. Then, later, on our way home, God kept us off a flight that went down over the Indian Ocean. There were no survivors.

In 1979, John was born. Eight days later, on a windy, rainy night, my dad went to the road to remove a tree limb after a passing motorist came to the farmhouse. While on the road, an intoxicated driver hit and killed my dad. That night, my grandfather, who had already buried two sons, accepted Jesus as his Savior. Although my grandfather was an upright, good citizen, I had prayed since I was very young for his salvation. In the depths of my sorrow at the loss of my dad, I was relieved my grandfather had become a Christian.

Doors continued to open to us. We were welcomed into the Association of Baptists for World Evangelism's (ABWE's) 1980 missionary candidate class. Although we thought we would be headed back to Bangladesh to help at the hospital we had visited, we listened to a missionary, Dal Washer, speak of the great need for medical missionaries in Togo, West Africa. God pierced our hearts, and we felt Togo was where we needed to go. We started raising support. By 1981, the support money had been raised, and we were headed to language school in Canada, a preparation stage that would impact more than we could have anticipated.

And all along the way, I wrote letters to my mom.

Part One: Language School in Canada

Before we were on our journey to Togo, we planned to spend one year in Canada to learn French and prepare for our trip. This, unexpectedly, turned into a couple of years. In 1981 we were in Sherbrooke, in southern Québec, and then in 1982, we moved to Québec City.

In our first year, after a family bout with the flu, I never recovered. The doctors diagnosed it as mononucleosis which became encephalitis. This illness held on for months and then years. It halted my language study. It gave me headaches, a general unwell feeling, fatigue, and created problems with my eyes. With four boys running around, I needed the help and support of those around me.

I spent a lot of time in prayer, not able to do much else, unsure of what God wanted from me. I was unable to study French for long periods, but as I slowly gained energy, I found a ministry all my own: letters. We received so many cards and letters each day. It became my goal to share with friends and family in Michigan and elsewhere all of what God was teaching me. More often than not, their letters encouraged me!

This extended stay was an opportunity for all of us to spend more time in the French language. At their young ages, the boys, especially, had a lot of energy and wonder. When we arrived in Sherbrooke, Luke was eight years old; Matthew six; Joshua was five; and John was just a toddler at two years old.

Through our stay in Canada, our family discovered how we could cope with transitions, and I saw how much I needed God in my day-to-day struggles.

September 1981 Newsletter

For God is not unjust so as to forget your work and the love which you have shown toward His name, by having served and by still serving the saints. Hebrews 6:10

Bonjour Mom,

Greetings from the beautiful country of Canada. After months of praying and planning, it seems like a miracle to really be here at language school. Learning French!

We are now settled in a cozy, five-room apartment on the pine-covered hillside of Sherbrooke. Josh calls it "our" motel. Luke and Matt are attending French public schools all day while Josh is in Beginners with a half-day of English and half-day of French instruction. Our hearts ache for those little guys who are a little bewildered trying to make friends and understand what's happening at school. However, we know in just a few months they will be teaching us French.

John stays at Bethel Bible Institute while Bob and I are in our French classes. Today, our French teacher told us that French is a heavenly language: it takes an eternity to learn it!

It's so peaceful and quiet here. (No emergency rooms calling!) What a tremendous year we've had seeing God's hand at work in our lives (and your life) to put us one big step closer to sharing the Good News in Togo.

Now on to this year of studying and learning!

Love,

Shirley

September 7, 1981

Dear Mom,

Bob had a beautiful opportunity to witness today during lunch hour. The girl is curious. *If the Togolese need to accept Christ as Savior, does she, too?* Bob is really excited about getting the French biblical terms memorized so he can share more. What great incentive.

Boys still do not catch the bus in the morning. Don't know why they miss it. I must be misunderstanding something with my limited French.

Josh is having problems in school. We see that he has a different way of learning. When I work with Josh at home, he only recognizes the letter *A,* and we're only looking at *A* through *G.* The school did some preliminary tests, so we'll talk with that lady and see what they recommend. It's times like these that make it so hard to be away from home, especially because I don't have a good understanding of French.

Luke has been busy at school. He has a computer class, and he came home and taught himself the complete typewriter keyboard just to get ahead.

Love,

Shirley

October 5, 1981

Dear Mom,

I sent off about ten letters to find out where we can get some French tracks, Bibles, and teaching aids to take to Togo. The answers are beginning to come back now. I will have to sit down and go through the information to see where we can get the most for our money.

Love,

Shirley

November 22, 1981

But thanks be to God, who always leads us in triumph in Christ, and through us reveals the fragrance of the knowledge of Him in every place. For we are a fragrance of Christ to God among those who are being saved and among those who are perishing: to the one an aroma from death to death, to the other an aroma from life to life. And who is adequate for these things?
2 Corinthians 2:14-16

Dear Mom,

What a precious, sweet scent the Cropsey house has experienced again this past month. So many have shared themselves with us in special ways during my recent illness. About a month ago, we had a bout with the flu. Nothing too exciting. Gastrointestinal. I had it for a couple of days and then Matt had it, too. Only I never recovered, so the virus and I (perhaps viral meningitis) continue to struggle. It seems to be lodged securely in my neck, and I stay in bed most of the time.

Micheline is the French-speaking girl I now read with each day. She lives in our apartment complex. We had a special need and God supplied it with Micheline who comes often to clean and bake, all in French, of course! So my French learning goes on using God's methods, our home continues to run smoothly (with lots of help from Bob, too), and I have had lots of time to get to know Micheline.

Last Friday I was exhausted after a long day of doctors and medical tests. We came home to find Micheline making cookies, looking depressed. She said, "Oh, I think I go to church with you Sunday. OK?"

Instead of just saying yes and going to bed, I continued the conversation, "Micheline, you know you don't have to go to church to get your relationship with God straightened out?"

She looked at me wide-eyed.

"Let's sit down, and I'll show you God's plan for each of us from God's Word," I said.

I watched as God drew a child unto Himself and then heard that child accept. It never stops being exciting! We have a new baby sister in Christ.

Pray for her. She attended church this morning and knows she needs to read her Bible and pray. She also knows she needs to grow and share Christ with others. I now have a responsibility of equal importance, to continue to show her Christ through my actions and words.

We need special wisdom to discern how to continue in our struggle to learn French and also how best to help her. She knows a lot more English than I do French but not necessarily "Christian terms."

God has an answer and solution to accomplish all.

Love,

Shirley

December 1, 1981

One who dwells in the shelter of the Most High

Will lodge in the shadow of the Almighty.

I will say to the LORD, "My refuge and my fortress,

My God, in whom I trust!" Psalm 91:1-2

Dear Mom,

I am feeling better and praying that I'll regain my strength and use what God gives me to accomplish my responsibilities in their respective order. Pray that I'll have the energy to study a couple of hours each day after quiet time. I need to start "doing" and being the wife and mother again this week because it is back to school again after Thanksgiving break. On Friday, the doctor said to rest a couple of more weeks. Missing six weeks of language school doesn't sound good to my logic, but God knows and His timing will be perfect. God called us to Togo. I believe He will accomplish it.

Love,

Shirley

P.S. Full responsibility of the boys has put an extra burden on Bob, stealing time from studies. How I praise the Lord for his positive attitude and thankful spirit through all of this time. He is a very special husband. The boys continue to live life to its fullest! And the best news? Due to budget cutbacks, dad's insistence, and John's cooperation, we are now a NO diaper household.

January 13, 1982

Dear Mom,

I thought it interesting that the Holy Spirit pointed me to this verse after talking to you: According to my earnest expectation and hope, that I will not be put to shame in anything, but that with all boldness, Christ will even now, as always, be exalted in my body, whether by life or by death. Philippians 1:20

Please pray that I surrender my will to Him absolutely daily. I've searched my heart and soul asking the Holy Spirit to point out any sin that may be the cause of my illness. I feel confident that is not it.

Hebrews 11:8 says, "By faith Abraham, when he was called, obeyed by going out to a place which he was to receive for an inheritance; and he left, not knowing where he was going."

I sure do not know what I'm going to do here this semester or in Togo, but I do know that God knows what He is doing—so my attitude must be to trust God entirely. I'm glad He doesn't let us know what He has planned next; He just continues to reveal who He is. Some days I feel alone here, but being alone with God isn't bad either. My solitude with Him has been special.

Mom, you are such a special person, a real testimony to me of God's love. I've seen you be faithful to Him through life's circumstances, and it has helped me often. I love you. This doesn't mean it is easy, right?

I count my blessings when I think of the chronic problems of so many people. But again, God makes special people out of individuals through illness, and there is a special blessing for those willing to help and encourage those "handicapped" for whatever reason.

I am rambling. Will go rest before dinner now. I've been doing simple, make-ahead, stick-in-the-oven meals. Bob does breakfast and lunch. The boys have been dolls in helping, so we are rewarding them with part of the money you gave us. The boys do the daily chores: make beds, pick up rooms, dust, vacuum, clear and set table, etc. So now I just need someone to do the floor, mirrors, bathroom, some baking, etc.

Boy, it is so easy to be replaced these days. Ha!

Love,

Shirley

February 1982 Newsletter

Dear Mom,

IT'S INCREDIBLE! IT'S A MIRACLE! Yes, God is still proving the things that are impossible with men are possible with Him (Matthew 19:26, Luke 1:37). The remaining $414,000 for the Togo hospital has been raised. We are now waiting for construction to get underway. Over $500,000 worth of donated medical supplies and equipment weighing a total of 150 tons is arriving in Togo. Truly, God does exceedingly and abundantly above all that we ask or think. Dr. Clutts is, at this very time, in Togo finalizing the construction plans with a national Christian contractor. Continue to pray!

Micheline has moved to Ottawa where she is involved in a Bible study. Pray for her continued growth with the Lord as we continue to follow up by mail.

After two months of continuing fatigue, stiff neck, blurring vision, etc., doctors in Michigan discovered that I have viral encephalitis (inflammation of the brain) and mononucleosis. I was advised to hold off on further language study until my health improved. Now, after three months, there is some slow, steady improvement!

Allow me to share from my heart. This "light affliction" (2 Corinthians 4:17-18) has given way to great blessing but not without searching and struggling on my part. God has given me a greater desire for His Word, to know Him better, and to practice the presence of God in my daily walk. I can count it a privilege to be sick knowing God has allowed it. I don't know what will be accomplished through it, but I trust that my Father knows what He is doing. He doesn't tell us what tomorrow holds, but He shows me more each day of who He is. I, being so unworthy, am bathed in His love and His peace. His grace was sufficient today, and I trust His promises; it will be sufficient tomorrow.

Love,

Shirley

April 4, 1982

Bonjour!

John decided on Saturday to start sucking his thumb. He was naughty in 55 ways, so I kept him home today to balance all the discipline with some love. He is a normal little guy!

I had Bob's phonetics teacher and her family over for dinner. All of the family speaks French. I was apprehensive about it, but it was just fine. We had a good evening, and the boys switched to French to talk to the children. I could usually figure out what was happening.

Mom, we just want to be in Togo when God wants us to be there! If we feel He's telling us not to go in September, we won't go. But on the other hand, I'm not hesitant to go with what I have now. There is no treatment, and I've not done well here. Satan will not win because of my health. God will help us as we remain in His will. You keep telling me we must claim God's control in all circumstances. I already don't like goodbyes or as the hymn says, "Blessed be the ties that bind," but then God hasn't said I would love it all! He'll give the grace to do what He asks us to do for Him.

If we stayed, Bob would take more French at the University of Laval, but we also must think about the boys and their schooling. The options are not simple at this point.

Bob should be home soon. I baked this morning. Josh and his friends are trying to make money. They "cleaned" for me. They got a screw caught in the vacuum and broke a belt. Expensive help, but they are trying. They had a yard sale from stuff they got out of the junkyard and fixed up. What industrious kids. Ha. I must praise the Lord for my boys and the good attitudes they maintain most of the time.

Gas stations are closed here because of the protest of gas surtaxes. It has become a dangerous situation. Bob got gas Saturday, so we are okay for a while.

Better close. Take care. We love you.

Love,

Shirley

April 22, 1982

Dear Mom,

Matthew came home from school yesterday with his face all scratched up from a fight. Luke said the kid just walked up and started hitting him. Then the boy finished it off by throwing stones. Bob will have to locate the kid if it keeps up. Or perhaps I should start picking them up from school? God, what is the right thing to do?

Luke came home with his report card. It hasn't changed much. He did get a nice comment from the teacher about his conduct and also his interest in school. But you can imagine how hard it is for Luke who is a very bright boy. He's used to being at the top of his class and now, in contrast, to be hardly passing his classes.

Ella, from Calvary, has gotten our food situation for Togo under control. She got the jars washed and has borrowed a tin can canner. We are going to purchase one for future use.

What a job! Sandy just picked up 2,000 packets of Kool-Aid for us so that will take a few minutes to repack.[1]

Love,

Shirley

May 27, 1982

Dear Mom,

You know, I've grown to really enjoy this little apartment, and I know it is because I've had such special times with the Lord here. It's time I've had because of illness. A verse that popped out is "But He knows the way I take; When He has put me to the test, I will come out as gold." (Job 23:10)

Job talks about looking for God, knowing he had done all God commanded, and yet not finding Him. It's not an easy chapter to just read without relating to it on so many different levels!

Mom, do you remember when I told you about Matthew and how he was getting beat up coming home from school each day? Well, when his grandmother Marian was here, she told him he should just turn around and punch the kid in the nose.

That is exactly what Matthew did and all of that ruckus coming home from school each day has stopped.

Love,

Shirley

June 2, 1982

Dear Mom,

I have thought much about this poem this week:

He Maketh No Mistake By A. M. Overton, 1932[2]

My Father's way may twist and turn

My heart may throb and ache,

But in my soul I'm glad to know,

He maketh no mistake.

My cherished plans may go astray,

My hopes may fade away,

But still I'll trust my Lord to lead,

For He doth know the way.

Tho' night be dark and it may seem

That day will never break,

I'll pin my faith, my all, in Him,

He maketh no mistake.

There's so much now I cannot see,

My eyesight's far too dim,

But come what may,

I'll simply trust and leave it all to Him.

For by and by the mist will lift,

And plain it all He'll make,

Through all the way, tho' dark to me,

He made not one mistake

I think my tolerance level is getting lower. My head pressure is still there, and I feel so tense. I'm just tired of not being well, I guess.

No news.

Bob is at church. I need to get the boys in and cleaned up. Matt has lots of homework, and John didn't get a nap.

Love,

Shirley

June 7, 1982

Dear Mom,

I got up this morning and felt almost normal! The head pressure was really beginning to get to me. Thank you, Lord!

Love,

Shirley

June 23, 1982

I wait for the LORD, my soul waits,

And I wait for His word. Psalm 130:5

Dear Mom,

Nothing could be truer for us as it appears that the Lord has placed us in a temporary holding pattern. Unless the Lord has a miracle in mind for restoring my health, we believe the Lord would have us remain here in Canada. Just within the last few weeks, I have experienced more fatigue and headaches than usual.

Whenever difficulties come into our lives, we are in danger of questioning God. We are discovering that instead there must be an attitude of complete reliance on God which results in an unnatural, unfathomable peace (Isaiah 26:3).

As we obey our heavenly Father despite the difficulties, our trust in Him actually increases as we watch Him unravel our problems and use them to His honor and glory.

Love,

Shirley

We spent the summer break in Michigan with family and friends. When we returned to Canada, we moved to an apartment in Québec City, not far from the St. Lawrence River.

October 5, 1982

Greetings from beautiful Québec City!

I am finding it impossible to enter into the French lifestyle once again: moving, unpacking, and maintaining peace and order with four boys and Bob— also fitting in needed rest with all the outside responsibilities—it has all been too much! So to cut back on many hours of correspondence, I have decided to type a few paragraphs of news that will be of interest to most of you (sorry for the impersonal approach).

Our summer was very exciting. We were able to keep all of our scheduled meetings throughout the summer months. God also answered prayer and helped us get most of our personal packing done as well as some of the hospital's packing. Thank you to each one who was so willing to become a part of the Togo ministry in the realm of packing, purchasing, building crates, donating, and caring for the Cropsey boys. *Merci beaucoup*! Thanks much!

Bob took a placement exam and was back in language school full-time beginning August 31. He is at a meeting tonight to learn how to better share our faith with the French on-campus. The boys are enrolled in the protestant public French school for the fall.

Lord willing, I will go to night school two evenings a week, each two and a half hours long. My doctor was very encouraged this summer and has given the green light to increase my activity slowly. I know. We don't seem to have medium speed. You're right! So now you know how to pray. I know it is one of my faults. I must try with God's help and wisdom to do all for His glory.

I need to remember this quote: "Urgent things are seldom important—important things are seldom urgent."[3]

Love,

Shirley

P.S. Mom, this is my personal note to you. I sent out 30 of these letters today, so I'm sort of caught up again. See, I took your advice.

October 7, 1982

Dear Mom,

John decided he had better ask Jesus into his heart this morning.

We were talking about bones and it just came up naturally. "Bones are there, but you can't see them. Kind of like Jesus. He is there, but you can't see him."

After he prayed, he said, "Oh, now there's two of us in there!"

Kids are great.

Love,

Shirley

November 16, 1982 Newsletter

Sainte-Foy, Québec (Just outside Québec City)

Dear Friends,

Just a little over a year ago, we began language school here in Canada, and we praise the Lord for His work of grace in our lives, drawing us closer to Him through some difficult times.

Humanly speaking, it is difficult to acknowledge defeat in a God-given goal. For me, that defeat is language school. God was good to remind me of Philippians 1:20 after we returned from the States last Christmas. It says, "According to my eager expectation and hope, that I will not be put to shame in anything, but that with all boldness, Christ will even now, as always, be exalted in my body, whether by life or by death." Even in my time of illness, God desired to receive the honor and glory!

Returning to Canada last winter, I didn't know what I'd do, but God knew what He was doing. It turned out to be a winter of very special communion with Him, sprinkled with the blessings of a unique outreach including corresponding with many of you and being able to be a part of local friends' lives.[4]

Psalm 119:71 says, "It is good for me that I was afflicted, So that I may learn Your statutes."

I had fleeting moments. Hours of dozing mixed with hallucinations. Strange dreams and mixed-up thoughts drove me to prayer. I was reminded of Psalm 119:76. It says, "May Your favor comfort me, According to Your word to Your servant."

God *was* merciful to me. God has returned my sight. I can hear higher-pitched sounds. My neurological tests are normal. I still tire very easily and have a great heaviness in the base of my skull with pressure in my ears. I remain with the expected side effects of poor memory, etc., but I am still willing to give all that God has left me!

After further consultation with doctors and with the home office, we will wait until the first of June before departing for Togo in order to maximize any further recovery that I may yet make in a good climate. Neither Bob nor I sense that God is changing His call in our lives, even though God has made us very aware that we must be as willing to stay home and serve Him as we are to go. We still believe, even with my physical limitations, that we can be an effective part of the medical evangelism ministry in Togo.

In the meantime, we will continue our French studies here, and we remember the words of Isaiah 6:8, "Then I heard the voice of the Lord, saying, 'Whom shall I send, and who will go for Us?' Then I said, 'Here am I. Send me!'"

Oh, to go to Togo!

Love,

Shirley

P.S. Mom, Bob had the flu and stayed in bed for a couple of days. I felt great last week and rather liked the switch, but Bob didn't laugh! He is fine now.

Oh, Mom, Grandma Shannon has been really encouraging me with Scripture in her letters. It seems like God is giving just a bit of that special inheritance He speaks of in His Word.[5] I praise the Lord you are so willing to talk and share with the boys about biblical subjects. It is such a special part of being a grandchild—just spending time with a grandparent—and time in God's Word.

November 22, 1982

Dear Mom,

Bob and I were talking. We decided that we have really not been teaching the boys what it is to pray. The other night, Bob explained how to pray the acronym ACTS: Adoration, Confession, Thanksgiving, and Supplication. It is a delight to hear how the boys give adoration to God, what they feel they need to confess, their thanksgiving to God, and what they are burdened to request. It makes me take notice of my own prayers.

John decided the other morning that perhaps he better not go to heaven. Like any parent, my heart sank, but I asked him why he wanted out! He said because he might fall out of heaven. He didn't see any boards up there in the sky to hold him in! So we looked at some verses that tell about heaven and that Jesus is preparing a place for us now.

Then he wanted to know just where is it then?

I said, "We don't know, but Jesus does."

He seemed content. The next day he was playing with his little toy people and pretending that they were in the desert. I told him that's where some of our missionary friends were telling people about Jesus. I then asked him if that was our mission. He said no because we didn't know where heaven was anyway! I sat down with him again and assured him that Jesus always cares, and he's making provisions to care for us. He promises to have a special place and how nice it will be for us.

How I thank the Lord for this time to spend with John! I can listen to some of the things that concern him. I am a miserable failure at answers, but then I must accept my own words and ask God for wisdom. He promises to give it liberally!

I seem to be sliding downhill again. I was given some advice and will take some medication in hopes that it will help break me out of this cycle of up and down. When my brain swells, I have many symptoms, and it is difficult to function.

The trick is to keep my brain from swelling. I am praying this treatment will help. Pray God will keep me from being discouraged.

Love,

Shirley

January 6, 1983

Bonjour Mom!

The suitcases are unpacked, the apartment is sparkling (the establishment painted and shampooed the carpets over the holidays!), and apple pies are in the oven. John is napping, and the other boys are not due home for another hour. It is always great to travel and visit Michigan, but it is a good feeling to be settled back into a schedule and be home again.

The boys were all a bit apprehensive to return to school after being away for three weeks. They all came home smiling and happy to be reunited with their friends. Matthew has had the most difficult time leaving family and friends back in Michigan. Would you pray with us for the necessary adjustments as we continue to seek God's will in our lives?

The washer set I have had since we came here broke down for the last time. Bob went out and replaced it with a different set yesterday! The delivery guys are here right now, so we will see what these new beauties can do for us. Laundromats are scarce and very expensive here. There isn't any place in the apartment to wash, so we just look at this purchase as another experience in practicing our French.

The boys are enjoying the sport of ice skating. They have a large rink over at the park. Also, the tennis courts all froze over due to the weather, so they are a great ice rink replacement when the bigger kids take the real rink over.

French language school starts next Monday for the big people here. Bob is planning to go to evening classes and work at the church and with a surgeon. Thank you, Lord, for working out all of the details. It will take discipline to make these practical experiences the optimum learning for him. I have a twice-a-week tutor.

Thank you so much for all of the food. I gave you credit for the spinach last night. The boys weren't too impressed with it. Think I'll try making a quiche with it next time!

I counted my correspondence for the first of the week. 157! And we have gotten 10-20 letters every day! God is so good to keep us encouraged.

Thank you for a beautiful Christmas.

Love,

Shirley

January 23, 1983

Mom,

The strike is on so the boys are off school again.

All the boys' teachers sent homework to do during the strike. I was so pleased. I'd gone on Monday to ask, and they said no. They would not send books home. But prayer changes things, and God knows my boys need to keep on working. God even made it better than my original request: *All* of the students got homework, so ours didn't have to feel different again.

It is late. I wrote letters all day today, and my little finger is cramping up. Take care.

Love,

Shirley

February 24, 1983

Dear Mom,

It is a beautiful sunny day here. Yesterday the boys were sent home in the morning because we were having a blizzard! We got a couple of inches of snow with lots of blowing. By night, the roads were fine, and we went to church.

I must be getting better or I've dropped off the deep end! My friend Sandy, who is also in language school, came this morning as usual and somehow I ended up with all her kids this weekend. She said they'd be leaving tomorrow and coming back Sunday. They took the train to Saskatchewan. I know the Lord will help me because I need His strength. Joy is two years old, David three, KK is five, and Nathan is six.

We got shots on Tuesday—two each. John did so well on the first and then he fell apart crying, "But I just wanted one!" He wasn't prepared for two! I had a good reaction to one of them.

The boys are off school next week for spring break. It doesn't sound like the teachers are going to settle. They are back for a three-week cooling off, and then they will strike again. The university is going on strike next week, too. All of the unions have united to support the teachers, so we could have a real shutdown.

Joy is still napping but everybody else is up. The boys will all be home in about 20 minutes.

I'd better close and get supper going. I'll do my best to keep one step ahead of the gang.

Love,

Shirley

March 8, 1983

Dear Mom,

Josh's teacher called. They are doing more extensive testing. He doesn't remember his alphabet! They put him in a starter reader, and he's going extra to read to another person. He really lacks self-confidence now, so pray. He is becoming more and more negative because he doesn't succeed as the others do. He reads his story often enough in the evening so he has it memorized, but he is not really reading it. It breaks my heart.

I've written letters all day. The mail came, and we received more than I wrote! It is an encouragement to us and always worth the time, many times over!

I am reading in the book of Numbers. What a holy God we serve!

Love,

Shirley

March 15, 1983

Dear Mom,

Just wanted to get a note in with this card.

John got his whole hand caught in the back door at church Sunday night. The boys couldn't get the door open, and they were all frantic by the time it was out! A man came and got it open, and we put John's hand in the snow right away. Other than a couple of bruises, it seems fine. Praise the Lord because it should have been crushed! On the way home, John wanted to know what would happen now. I told him God made us unique, and it would heal. Josh asked him on the way into the house how he was, and he said, "I am sealing! God made me unique." He has come up with some real winners lately.

Boys are back in school for a couple of weeks again. Strike not settled. Better close.

Love,

Shirley

March 1983 Newsletter

Dear Mom,

THE COUNTDOWN IS ON! We're T-minus 50 days and counting (depending on when you get this letter)! Having been bitten by the BCG (tuberculosis vaccine), yellow fever, typhoid, and hepatitis B vaccines—with passports in hand—ALL systems are GO for liftoff from Montreal to Togo on May 14.

How we have had "grace of the Lord Jesus Christ, and the love of God, and the fellowship of the Holy Spirit" (2 Corinthians 13:14) during this past year as God has prepared us for the immense task that lies before us! We are especially thankful that my health has continued to improve since Christmas.

We're ready to go to Togo!

Love,

Shirley

April 20, 1983

Dear Mom,

  I have been writing letters this evening and decided I'd better jot you a note.

  As the last days pass before we leave, God gives peace through His Word. I often turn back to Deuteronomy 31:8 that says, "The Lord is the one who is going ahead of you; He will be with you. He will not desert you or abandon you. Do not fear or be dismayed."

  Today I'm dwelling on Isaiah 55:12*a*, "For you will go out with joy And be led forth in peace."

  I know I must go giving thanks and praise to the Lord. What a privilege it is to be a part of the King's army and to take up the cross and follow as He leads. I am so unworthy.

  I must close. The clock is coming up on midnight. Makes a difference when I can't sleep until 9 a.m.!

Love,

Shirley

May 2, 1983

Dear Mom,

  Did I tell you about my haircut? I asked to have a little cut off, and I just have a little hair left! Oh me, I'm not so good in French yet, but it is a cute cut.

Got our last shots last night. John was sick, but he is okay now. We are all sporting sore arms. Bob has given me the second-degree about resting again. I do try, but some days I just don't do so well as others.

Our tickets came yesterday for Togo! This is really happening!

Love,

Shirley

Part Two: Our First Year in Togo

Our first year in Togo was full of adjustments. Not only were we adjusting to a new climate and culture, but we were also figuring out what God had for us in Togo. We spent that first year learning the local language, Ewe (pronounced ay-vay), and finding our way.

The first step, for me, was establishing our home. We started off staying with another missionary family, then moved into a temporary place that a missionary family had recently vacated. Then on to our "in-between" house, which we rented until our house on the hospital compound could be built.

Once our home was set up, it was figuring out "how" to run our household with spotty electricity and the many creatures, great and small, who were not a part of our daily life in Canada or Michigan! Fortunately, we had tremendous national house help who assisted me with the daily washing, food prep, etc., but who also became treasured friends and our cultural brokers. I was able to visit villages and share the gospel with our village neighbors because of these special friends.

Another source of friendship was with our fellow missionaries. I was delighted to pour into and have others pour into me. However, although we had a common goal of reaching the Togolese people through medical missions, not every missionary had the same idea of how to go about it. This caused interpersonal strife, and we had to pray and work through different struggles as we learned the art of conflict management our first year. As with any organization, when you put a lot of people together, then add pressure and stress, not everyone agrees. However, God proved bigger than our struggles. When we sought Him, a resolution came forth.

Throughout that first year, God brought us reminders of home and showed us his love. We went through phases of homesickness. It was especially burdensome when loved ones in the States died, and we were unable to mourn with family and friends. However, God was our comfort. I found ways to make holidays and birthdays special by creating unique cakes. Friends from the States were also generous by sending small gifts or special foods through the mail or our containers shipped from the U.S.

I continued my ministry of letters and found a ministry in hospitality. We had our national Christian friends, other missionaries, and short-term missionaries who all came through our door. By the end of the year, I felt comfortable serving a proper African meal, so we were inviting national officials whom Bob worked with outside of the hospital into our home.

My health, which had delayed us in coming to Togo, continued to be our biggest concern. Like a yoyo, my health went up and down. The burden of keeping up the house, even with extra help, challenged me—along with all the additional activities we participated in, which included being part of the church plant in a nearby village, leading the school committee, and being part of the hospital decisions. There was always something to think about and something that needed to be done. Yet, I learned that if I didn't rest, I was even less effective.

Our first year of Togo was full of lessons in setting boundaries and knowing where to pour our energy—physical, emotional, and mental—in an effort to give God all the glory.

Places

HBB, although mostly referred to as just the "hospital," HBB stands for *Hôpital Baptiste Biblique.* (Its French name.) In English, it is called the Karolyn Kempton Memorial Christian Hospital. HBB was the hospital in the South and the first Togo hospital ABWE built. It is near Adeta.

Kpalimé is a large city about 25 miles from HBB. I did weekly shopping there, and the Blind Center was located just outside of it. This was the first city where we lived until HBB had housing for us.

Kpodzi is the village where we worked as church planters with a new graduate of the Bible Institute in Lomé, Pastor Paul.

Lomé is about 120 miles from Kpalimé. Although it took several hours to get there, this is where we did a lot of shopping (stores with imported items), ate at restaurants, and did other official business. The port was located here.

Agou was the home of Agou hospital where we took Luke and Matt (with their injuries) before HBB was built. It was established by the Germans.

Bethania was a hotel, pool, and restaurant where we went to relax. Field council and other meetings were held there. The boys loved it when we went because they had french fries on the menu (and often had actual potatoes to make them). This is also where the boys contracted schistosomiasis from playing "king of the hill" off paddle boats in a polluted pond.

Fellow Missionaries

Steve and Martha Anderson, by profession, were nurse and teacher, respectively. They had three children. They were church planters and lived on the HBB compound. We knew them from our language study time at Sherbrooke, and they were a familiar face when we landed in Togo.

Dr. Dave and Kathy Clutts were long-term missionaries. Dave designed and oversaw the building of HBB before he functioned as a doctor and surgeon. They lived near the village of Adeta until HBB built their house on the HBB compound.

Jim and Ellen Livingston were short-termers. Jim Livingston was a carpenter and worked on the construction of HBB. Ellen helped at the Mission Kid (MK) school.

"Uncle" Dave Muller was a young, unmarried short termer who came out to work during hospital construction. He spent lots of time with our boys. He lived in the guardian house, which he built of stone, before the hospital hired a full-time guard.

Ardene Nunn was a short-term MK teacher for two years.

Kelli Thayer came to teach short-term and turned into a career MK school teacher.

Dal and Kay Washer were experienced missionaries who were instrumental in opening the mission field of Togo. As career church planting missionaries, their ministry was the Blind Center. As our senior missionaries, they helped us with Togolese culture, customs, and all the details of how to live in Togo.

Denny and Diane Washer were church planters. Denny was also a pilot. Denny was the son of Dal and Kay Washer.

Ron and Ann Washer were career church planters. Bradley and Melissa were their children and good friends with our boys, especially John. Ron was the son of Dal and Kay Washer.

Peggy Williams was a career missionary who ministered at the Blind Center.

Nationals

You will notice that several of the Togolese names are similar. Children are named based on the day they are born. If there are several in the family born on the same day, you add a "ga" for an older sibling and a "vi" for a younger sibling.

Adzovi was our house help and friend. I had a short devotional and prayer with her before we began our day, almost every day. When we hired her, she moved to Kpalimé to work for us. She also followed us to the hospital. In time, she married Justin. As a believer, she became an excellent friend and co-laborer in the gospel. She taught me so much about the culture. We did village visitations together, and she was always with me when I represented Bob at funerals, weddings, church work, and even one day, in court.

Mr. Divine and Mercy Dzagli were both dear friends, spoke English, and named two of their children Shirley and Bob! They came to Kpalimé about the time we arrived and decided to follow Jesus. Divine was our language teacher and after HBB opened, became the main lab director. He was an evangelist. They moved to Tsiko, the small village near the hospital, around the time HBB opened. I was privileged to have a weekly Bible study with Mercy.

Kofi was our yard worker and errand boy while living in Kpalimé, but he would also do anything that needed to be done.

Pastor Paul was a new graduate of the Bible Institute. We worked with him on a church plant in the village of Kpodzi.

Salome lived just in front of the Kpalimé church. She was still in school when we arrived. She spoke excellent English.

May 26, 1983

(85% humidity, 87 degrees)

Dear Mom,

I think we last visited (via the phone) on the marvelous Air Africa flight! That plane lacked in all areas of quality. I can't remember if I shared about the man and child sitting next to me. He was giving his small child, who looked about twenty months old, beer to drink. Then he spilled it all over me! I smelled very suspicious after that incident! Ha!

We got off the airplane and were greeted by the Togo team. What a warm welcome! The whole group helped us, and we were through customs in no time. Bob accidentally put his briefcase down, and we thought we wouldn't see it again! But Mrs. Kay Washer just marched back into the restricted area. There it was sitting! Thank you, Lord!

All of our luggage arrived, and there isn't anything missing. Again, thank you, Lord! Our kids were delighted to see the Anderson family, whom they knew from our language study time in Sherbrook, Canada. The Andersons drove our suburban, which had been shipped earlier, to pick us up. The suburban was just another familiar sight to welcome us to this new place.

The whole welcome group went to the Neufeld's home for lunch before we drove from Lomé to Kpalimé, which is a 121-mile drive. It was great to give the boys a break and have a full tummy.

We are staying with the Andersons until our next place is ready for us. God has answered prayers in this situation. The kids are getting along very well, and so are we! The boys are all in a room, and we have a room.

It looks like we will move about three times this summer. When the Boonstras, who are short-term construction missionaries, leave to go home, we will move where they live now. Then we'll live in another house we call the "in-between" house before we eventually move to the house at the hospital. The house at the hospital hasn't been built yet, but the hospital's whole construction project is coming along.

I wish words could adequately express the thrill it was for us to see the hospital for the first time. The country is just like the pictures. We drove out to see the hospital site yesterday morning. Uncle Dave has done a great job. It looks so magnificent with all the beautiful flagstone exterior! All the roofing is now completed and the inside finish work is underway. We are hoping to open the doors of the hospital for business next summer when everyone has finished their Ewe language study, and the missionary homes are completed. Wow, we can hardly wait!

Tuesday, we had lots of company while Steve Anderson and Bob drove to Lomé. Steve needed to take care of a bad tooth. They got the run around all day and didn't accomplish much of anything. Welcome to Togo! Or WAWA (West Africa Wins Again)!

Church last night was trilingual. Dal Washer preached in English, which was interpreted into Ewe, the primary language here. We heard French in prayer requests and songs. I felt very comfortable being there and enjoyed the time. Next Sunday we will give our testimonies.

This morning I woke up with runny eyes and that bad taste in my mouth, so I am just resting. I don't think I'll go out at all.

Psalm 48:1*a* says, "Great is the LORD, and greatly to be praised." I think that sums up my thoughts for the afternoon. Remember, we love you and need you. We have been strengthened so much by your positive support!

Love,

Shirley

May 29, 1983

Dear Mom,

We have been in Togo for nearly a week. Our stay with the Anderson family has been a happy one. It has worked well to have meals at other missionaries' homes to become acquainted with our co-workers in Christ.

Yesterday we packed up the boys and drove to the pool at Bethania. It was so hot! The rainy season has just begun, so when the rain started, we let the kids swim in the rain because it wasn't storming.

We met the man who is building our "in-between" house, which we will live in until we move to the house on the hospital compound. I am so glad for the dressers and shelves we brought along. The kitchens here are small and have a sink. That's all. Period! I have cold running water in the kitchen. We are supposed to be there at 7:30 a.m. to tell the painter about the paint. All the floors are cement and painted a funny red color.

The boys are doing great. Josh is coming out of his "I can't" stage. He's become adventurous. He took off yesterday and went to the market with one of the missionary ladies.

John is in the first stage of adjustment. He came running from his class and sat on my lap and said, "I want to go home—to Grandma's. NOW!"

I asked him what was wrong.

"Nothing," he said. Then, silence. "I hate it here."

"Oh," I said. "I'm sorry. We'll have to pray about that together." And then he just cried.

We are all just trying to figure things out here.

Love,

Shirley

May 31, 1983

Dear Mom,

I stayed in bed until about 10:30 a.m. and slept this morning. Adzo, Martha's house help, took me to the market this afternoon. It is just like the pictures: people everywhere with their little piece or pan of goods for sale. I bought material to have an African dress made for myself. There is so much available in Lomé! Martha is letting me use her freezer, so I was able to get meat, too. It will give us a good start next week when we are on our own. I'll have appliances and even a wringer washer to use!

Martha will let Adzo help me clean on Saturday before we move into our temporary house, which is before our "in-between" house, which is still being constructed (and before our eventual house which is also still to be built on the hospital compound.)

Bob went to the "in-between" house and talked to the painter yesterday morning. I decided the boys' bedroom should be powder blue, and the rest just painted off white. Often what you say and what gets done are very different when dealing with Togo construction, so we'll see what happens.

We were at Washers again tonight. Dal gave us some orientation to different areas of Togo life. Meanwhile, the boys made a rope swing with the African houseboy. While helping, the houseboy fell out of the tree and nearly hung himself; his neck had a rope burn on it! But he is okay otherwise.

Need to close. Give our greetings to everyone.

Love,
Shirley

June 5, 1983 (Sunday afternoon, 3:15 p.m.)

Dear Mom,

We are now in our temporary home. Bob took the Boonstra family to Lomé on Friday, and we moved into their house Saturday morning.

I had Adzo, Martha's house help, come with me and work yesterday. Bob closed the house and sprayed it for bugs on Friday night, so I wanted to be safe and give it a good cleaning before we got too moved in. Adzo washed everything in the kitchen and resettled it. We also had another young boy work, and he washed clothes in the wringer washer, cleaned the garage, etc.

The house has all the appliances, including a small freezer. We are very thankful for the transformers and fans. They are the Washer family's appliances, and we will return them at the end of this month. Our things haven't arrived yet. But for now, we use theirs. I baked all day at Anderson's house last week and put cookies and a cake in the freezer. The cake is for Joshua's birthday. I'm going to try to make an apple pie out of mangoes. We have pineapples and bananas that are delicious. I can get potatoes, onions, eggs, and sweet bread, too. There is a lot available if you are willing to pay the price. Pop is cheaper to drink than Kool-Aid because sugar is expensive!

Washer's houseboy killed a baby python and a green mamba between our houses last night.

Last Thursday, we had our first African meal of fufu with chicken sauce, and rice and beans with peanut-chicken sauce. It wasn't bad.

The boys started going to school last Thursday. Ardene, who teaches at the Missionary Kid (MK) school, thought it would be suitable for everyone to get acquainted before she tests them. They are happier to be busy, especially since our things haven't arrived. Continue to pray for the boys as they make adjustments. John shook hands with Adzo's boyfriend last night. Then he turned and looked at his hand and with a big smile says to me, "I didn't turn Black!"

Mail has been slow. Bob just got back from the post office, and we got forwarded mail from Québec! I tried all last week to call you. It will be fantastic to hear your voice when I get through. There is only a four-hour time difference between the U.S. and Togo.

Love,

Shirley

June 9, 1983

Dear Mom,

I got up early this morning and got the wash done before breakfast. It was much better to do it in the early morning than in the 120-degree heat.

Several different evenings toward dusk, there have been clouds of bats flying to a nearby cave. They just keep coming and coming—strange!

Here are some other unusual things that have happened.

I cut the end of my finger on a tin can, so it is in a splint. It's my right hand. Matt got bit by a dog this morning, so we are watching the dog's behavior to see if we need to be concerned for rabies. The boys buried lizard eggs that Uncle Dave found at the hospital. They placed a can nearby, so we can check and watch the eggs hatch.

I'm having an African dress made, and the girl came on Tuesday to measure me and take the material. She doesn't use dress patterns but can do it from a picture! How talented!

I need to close and get supper on the table. Hope Bob gets ahold of you today. We keep trying. No mail from home yet.

Love,

Shirley

June 12, 1983

Dear Mom,

We just got our first letter from you yesterday. Boy, was I glad to hear from you!

Bob got us a wardrobe and bookshelves that will help with storage in our "in-between" house. Only two rooms have closets, and there isn't anything but a sink in the kitchen. We gave our landlord a three-month advance in rent so he could keep working on it. They have Dad's motto: If you have the money, you do it. If you don't have money, stop!

I had the privilege of sharing at the Blind Center on Friday. Before I started my talk, Kay had one of the girls come and give a tactile description of me so they knew how I looked. It was a real blessing to me. They had lots of special music, and it was beautiful. Today I've marked out the Romans Road[1] for a girl to take with her on vacation so her family can read the plan of salvation.

I've had diarrhea the last couple of days and a heavy head, so I just stayed in bed today. Martha's house help, Adzo, came yesterday and did the ironing[2] and some cleaning, too. She is a sweet girl.

There is a need for more rain. It is supposed to be the rainy season, but not much yet.

We love you so much.

Love,

Shirley

June 17, 1983 (78 degrees, 6 a.m.)

Dear Mom,

This note finds us in Lomé for orientation.

I am concerned about Matthew. His stomach has been upset on and off since we arrived, and now he has an itchy rash. Yesterday Bob went to the pharmacy to get me Flagyl for amoebic dysentery. He is having a list of drugs made up while we are here and will get Matt something for worms, I think.[3]

It was an exciting morning for Bob. The Kpodzi village Chief approached him, and Bob gave him a treatment. Then, while they were at the pharmacy, he met the man in charge of medicine over our area. On a side note, my medication has already helped me better acclimate.

Joshua had a super birthday! I took the Kpalimé kids, all 11 of them, to Bethania for swimming in the morning. We came back and roasted hot dogs and marshmallows. I decorated a cake with a giant alligator on it. It came out so cute, and Joshua was amazed. Our container hasn't arrived, but he got a couple of cards from the States.

I've enjoyed living near Kathy Clutts. She has a cheerful personality, and Suzanna is a content baby. The boys are good with Suzanna and enjoy playing with her. Since we share a courtyard, the boys also play with Clutts's parrot and Washer's monkey. We haven't gotten our own pet yet.

It is now 7:30 a.m., and the activity is picking up. We are supposed to be ready for breakfast at 8 a.m., so I'd better get in my cold shower! A cold shower feels pretty good when it is so hot outside. And to think, this is the cool season in Togo!

Love,

Shirley

June 25, 1983

Dear Mom,

Greetings from sunny, wet, humid Togo! We trust this letter will eventually get to you one of these days. Everyone was excited to receive all the things we shipped from the States in our container. It was quite a circus to see all the Africans helping. There were women and all their little children here to help also. It took Bob two days to load the container, but it only took two hours to unload with all the help. We are grateful!

Our "in-between" house is still not finished, but it is coming along Togo speed! Bob has been responsible for getting the extra things we *Yovos* (white people) think we need: screens, toilets, etc. Our landlord ran out of money—again—so the work stopped. That is an excellent financial philosophy, except we need a house. So we started with rent-advance allowances. We have now paid for our first year's rent in one way or another. Anyway, we hope to move into our new house sometime this week.

We were back at the church in Kpalimé this week. We have had the opportunity to visit many of the different ministries there. We also went last weekend to Lomé for four days of orientation. It was a refreshing time of fun and fellowship! We encountered many more new-to-us sights, smells, and sounds. It was most exciting to meet so many of the missionaries we heard about but had not yet met.

You can pray with us concerning house help. My French is pretty shaky. I'd like to work on the local language Ewe and just skip the French. Communication can be a real problem with a language barrier, so please pray that all will be as God plans and to His glory.

The national Christians are very gracious people and so patient with us. Salome has been helping me some and has begun to teach me a few words. She is trilingual and knows how to use the wringer washer!

The country is beautiful. We are in the rainy season now, and everything is green. It seems like you can stand and watch the tall grass grow. The rain has cooled the temperature down some, but it is still plenty humid, just like some of those hot, muggy days in Michigan.

Another big exciting day was our trip to the hospital site. Uncle Dave has done a fantastic job of being the all-around person for the construction. Another matter for prayer would be the future housing situation and where we all will be living eventually. It was such a blessing to see the water in the well, which we all prayed for in the past. Great is the Lord and much to be praised!

Bob made three trips to church this morning with the suburban packed with people. People are so open to the Word of God. The boys and I walked to church. It wasn't raining, and it was a beautiful day.

Trust this has given you a bit of an idea of what is happening.

Love,

Shirley

P.S. Could you send me U.S. stamps? Just a few each time you write? Also, I learned my first words in Ewe: sounds like *Octpay low* and means "thank you very much."

July 3, 1983

Dear Mom,

At last, we moved into our own place, which we will call our "in-between" house because it is "in-between" our stay at Boonstra's old home and our house built at the hospital. This "in-between" house isn't finished yet, but we are now able to unpack! Bob has been so good! He built shelves to organize the food and store toilet paper and everything else! I'm just sorting things into different bags now to get similar items together. We are so thankful for all that we brought, and it is so refreshing to see and use familiar things. I still haven't found any silverware, but I found some plastic utensils that work fine.

Mom, our "in-between" house is going to be so lovely when completed. I had them paint the walls off white, and the tile is brown. One of our rugs is wall-to-wall in the study-family room. All your oil pictures have made it thus far in good shape. The cupboard we got from the Neufelds fits just right in the kitchen! We got a pole placed in our closet today, and Bob put our water bed together. He is filling it now.

We only have hot water in our bathroom. The workers didn't finish the closets, nor the light fixtures, nor the painting. They do put us Americans to shame at making something from nothing, though! Dad would have loved it here in that respect.

I have been very pleased with my health. Keep praying as I can't get as much rest here with all the workers. They come at 6:30 a.m and stay until 4:00 p.m. (But still don't do much!)

The view out the back of our house is beautiful. It is a picture of splendor: tropical plants and trees with mountains in the distance.

We had ten extra for supper tonight. Have had company five times that amount this week, but no more for a while now. I've rested all day. Luke and I had a pop and a few treasured chocolate candies tonight and just talked. He is becoming a young man and a real friend.

Mom, I pray for you often. We are all homesick and trusting God to fill the empty spot as only He can do for us.

Philippians 4:19 says, "And my God will supply all your needs according to His riches in glory in Christ Jesus."

We have peace about being here and are content to rest in Him. Must close. We love you!

Love,

Shirley

July 17, 1983

Dear Mom,

This month is just flying by so quickly. Is that a sign of old age settling in on me?

It rained today. We needed it. Ironically, the rainy season has been dry! We drove to Lomé this morning for church. It was beautiful to look around, sitting at the edge of the village. The poverty was behind us, and the beauty of the jungle all around.

I started a Bible club tonight for the little people. The six smaller children are five years old and under. We had a good time together. John has surprised me in all he can do!

Our house help, Kofi, decided to check the oil in the generator Saturday before he turned it off. Oil sprayed the clothes on the line. But Praise the Lord, he and the generator are okay.

We got a dog Saturday. He is a worthless hot dog. A thief rode off on Luke's bike Saturday afternoon, and the dog didn't even bark! But today, he trapped an animal that looks like a large rat. The African kids killed the rat and will eat it. So if the dog keeps the critter population in the yard down, he will earn his meals. The boys are delighted!

Our house help, Adzovi, starts work tomorrow. Salome will stay part-time until school begins in the fall. It will surely help me to get all the hard cleaning done here.

Love,

Shirley

July 25, 1983

(11 a.m.)

Dear Mom,

Bob and Luke are at the hospital working today. Bob started going every day until language starts up in the fall. He leaves by 6:30 a.m. and gets back around 3 p.m. I think the little motorcycle at the hospital might be an incentive for Luke going. Ha!

Bob talked the plumbers into putting hot water into the kitchen in exchange for a pair of shoes. That was Saturday, and they are here this morning. They knocked holes all over the walls that just got painted! It will be nice when it's all finished, though.

The generator is going, and I can hear the plumbers with their hammers and chisel. What happened to the peaceful jungle noise?

Matt woke up from his nap with a 105 temperature and headache on Sunday. It may be our first malaria attack. He is at 102 this morning but is acting okay.

Will write more later.

Love,

Shirley

August 1983 Newsletter

Dear Mom,

GREETINGS FROM BEAUTIFUL TOGO! I wish words could adequately express how thrilled we are to be here. God has been so good to allow us to come to this lovely country. The people and the country are even more beautiful than I could have dreamed.

The boys love Togo! Luke says we should tell you about the green mamba and python snakes the nationals killed just outside our gate. Matt likes chasing the little lizards that are everywhere, and Josh has fallen in love with the monkey next door. John isn't too big on any of the creatures, great or small, but ask him how he likes Togo— "FINE," he says. Everyone seems to be adapting.

We are excited about the many opportunities to share Christ in our home, on the street corner, and house-to-house visitations. What a joy to share the gospel with people who are so open and eager to listen (and with no time constraints)! Because most women and children speak Ewe primarily, we are anxious to learn Ewe to better communicate the gospel to them.

It's the rainy season, and everyone is happy to see the much-needed rain. Kids are splashing each other in the mud puddles, women are carrying the big loads of wood, fruit, and vegetables to the market, and men are hoeing the corn in the mud. The road up the nearby mountain is steep, narrow, and washed out from the fresh rains that have brought new life to the countryside. We have a beautiful, panoramic view with banana, palm, and papaya trees, sprinkled with poinsettias, and clusters of wildflowers everywhere. It is a good land which the Lord our God doth give us! We are joyfully serving the King of Kings!

Love,

Shirley

August 4, 1983

Dear Mom,

Last Friday, we were in Lomé. I tried to call you around 9 p.m. The ring was so clear, but there was no answer. The drive back takes a couple of hours, so although we wanted to stay and try again, we needed to get back. (There is field council on Monday, so I'll try again.)

We shopped in the morning, and Bob had a couple of appointments. In the afternoon, we drove out to Lake Togo. The kids went swimming, and we stopped for a "banana split." At least, that's what they called it. (EVERYTHING is different!)

The boys have just had a ball at camp this week. It has been so good for them to mix with the nationals and just have fun. The missionary kids get pretty special treatment by Ron Washer and love it. Salome has been a full-time counselor at camp these two weeks. Adzovi is super helpful here, and all is working out. I'm learning French! God has given us super household help, which has enabled me to keep my head above water.

Tuesday, I stayed low most of the day. Every time I fell asleep, John did something naughty (a regular kid). He thinks he does not need to listen to the national help, so he rebels. It has initiated most of the spankings lately—PRAY.

Bob has been picking up between 25-30 people from the village of Kpodzi for church. He and Pastor Paul may start a church there.

The boys were in bed by 8:15 p.m. and Bob too. It is now 10:10 p.m. so guess I'll close and go to bed.

"For God so loved the world." John 3:16a

Love,

Shirley

September 12, 1983

Dear Mom,

School has now begun full time. The boys enjoyed their first couple of days. Josh was able to read his work. Matt will be the one who needs to learn self-discipline and practice reading too. He has Michelle Washer in his class, and she reads all the time. But he can sure ride that motorcycle!

We are in dire need of school teachers starting next year. Ardene has been so dedicated to the kids here. She stayed an extra year on her short-term time, so she needs some good teachers to come and replace her.

I got some preschool learning books out for John. He just isn't ready for school, so we'll take it at his pace.

Kpodzi village was a real blessing yesterday. We held our first church service. The Chief went forward for salvation as did more than 30 others. Only God knows their hearts, so pray. By the end, there must have been 120 people at the church service. We (Adzovi taught in Ewe) had 54 kids in a small 9x12 room. Bob would like the work to be in the hands of the nationals ultimately. The church's leader is Pastor Paul, a recent graduate of the Bible Institute and a mature Christian.

Dal Washer is doubtful if the church will work well without our help, so I don't know what will happen. He thinks Pastor Paul is too young and the people won't listen to him. Pray for discernment as we move forward. Also, pray for good discipleship programs to begin for these new Christians.

My Ewe language class this morning was good. I'd be delighted if I could just learn some greetings. There are three tones with a phonetic alphabet. Unlike French, you pronounce all the letters.

I'm looking out the window, past the full clotheslines, and the rain is coming over the mountains. Must go to save my dried clothes.

Love,

Shirley

September 21, 1983

"Have I not commanded you? Be strong and courageous! Do not be terrified nor dismayed, for the LORD your God is with you wherever you go."
Joshua 1:9

Dear Mom,

It is a beautiful day in the 80s with a breeze. Boy, did we get the rain last weekend! I took the wash up and down five times until I finally gave up.

This week, I continued with my two hours of language class with Bob each morning. I'll take it a week at a time and see how it goes. I have enjoyed it so far. On Mondays, I have three hours, and that is a bit much.

Bob brought our furniture back from Lomé. They didn't have it stained right, so he just paid them less. It looks nice, though. Our house is beautiful here. I am so comfortable and happy with it, Mom. Your oil paintings make it feel more like home. I'm happy I brought them out here.

My appliances are dropping off quickly. The washer won't spin out. We run it off the generator. The microwave quit again. Salome broke a piece off the food processor, but it still works.

The boys rearranged their rooms last night. Bob just told them to make a plan before they started. Well, they made a plan and put the bunk beds three high! I asked Bob to put up a rail so no one falls out, but it is still a bit much for me. MEN.

We now have our yard transplant done. Kofi planted hunks of grass all over, and it is supposed to make a grassy yard!

Take care. Your letters mean so much—thank you for writing so faithfully.

Love,

Shirley

September 26, 1983

Dear Mom,

The days go by so quickly here. I guess it is because one can never accomplish what you plan for a day. I haven't figured out how to be realistic yet, and I'm not sure why!

The new 100-pound bags of flour came in last week, so we have plenty. Best off, Salome's mother can make bread again because Bob got flour for her, too! We are happy with her bread, and it saves me a lot of time.

My washer isn't working right. It will not spin out, so we are back to using the wringer washer. Praise the Lord; it is available. We have at least twice the laundry because of dirt and heat. I have to do towels every other day, or they stink. It's just so hot and humid here!

I got hungry for a candy bar the other day, so I made my own version with rice crispies and chocolate chips. My version was not bad. I also made hot fudge and homemade ice cream for family night, and it was yummy! I've been trying to recreate something familiar each week. The boys enjoy it, too.

I started a study in Philippians this afternoon. I think it will be an excellent spiritual lift for me. If you don't seek your spiritual encouragement here, you sink. All the church services are in Ewe. This makes it hard to dig into the Word of God when you only understand every other word or so.

(Three people are calling me, so I guess I'll write later.)

Love,

Shirley

September 27, 1983 (Tuesday p.m.)

Mom,

Some guy got into our house last Saturday. He found me in the bedroom. I talked him into going out to the living room. He wanted money. His appearance was strange, like he was on drugs. Josh went and got Denny Washer because I couldn't get the man to leave. I was afraid to be forceful. I don't know where he came from, but Ghana is so close and so needy. Many soldiers are floating our way from there, so pray for all of us.

Last week, the Catholic group in Kpodzi put us out of the school where we were holding services. The Chief spoke up for us but was outnumbered in the vote. We (Pastor Paul, Bob, and I) want to stay in Kpodzi because the Lord is working. But instead of meeting at the school, the Chief gave us the back of his compound and his office. The attendance remained over 100! The Chief even had his best friend come, and he got saved! God encouraged us! We know God is at work when there is such opposition. Pray for the boys. Matt found some peanut shells and corn cob and built a space rocket launch during church on Sunday. We need God's wisdom to keep the boys interested and wanting to go to church, even if they don't understand the Ewe preaching. May the opposition be a positive thing to strengthen each of us!

I've been getting about 20 hours of class/study time each week. It sure puts a dent in all other activities. I miss Salome around here (both her help and her personality). She sent me the sweetest note before she left for school.

Love,

Shirley

October 4, 1983

Dear Mom,

I should be trying to study, but I didn't go to class this morning. John keeps talking. He needs attention, and I just didn't think it was right to leave him. I guess we are all homesick. I thought we'd made it over the hump, but the adjustments never stop.

There are men out working again today. They dug a very shallow hole to run the wire from the house for electricity. Nothing in the kitchen works anymore. The smaller appliances just haven't done well on the transformers.

The boys have heat rash. Josh also has some other skin rash on his head and back. It itches him. Bob started using a steroid cream, so pray it will help him.

I made a skirt for Salome. She started school, and I do miss her. I also made curtains to put over the shelves in the laundry room. I now need to make cushions for the extra chair we have to match our wickers.

We took off last Saturday morning just for a change. Drove to Bethania and spent a couple of hours in the pool. Then we went to the top of the highest mountain in Togo, Mountain Agou.

With all the interruptions, I see it is almost noon. I've been using the slow cooker a lot and have chicken, rice, and peas today. Trying to do our big meal at noon, but it takes some doing with school from 10 to noon. The boys need to be back by 1 p.m. Our house is about a five-minute walk down the road from the school.

Looks like rain again. We had a great shower last night! The wash is dry, so I'd better go take it down because the rain comes fast when it comes—quick and hard.

Take care.

Love,

Shirley

October 9, 1983

Dear Mom,

The Washers leave tomorrow for the States, so I decided to get a note off to you!

The harmattan season seems to be settling in here. The season is anywhere from October to the middle of March. It's a big, dusty wind from the Sahara Desert. I look out the window and can't see the mountain anymore. I hear it gets so dusty you can't see the back wall!

Yesterday was full. Bob and men from the Kpalimé church started to clear the land for our chapel at Kpodzi. Then, in the afternoon, the school had an open house. It was so lovely. Martha made a darling cake while Ann and I decorated. I also made punch, finger jello, and apple cookies. I used your "Christmas cookie" recipe. Yum! The kids did a darling program, and Bob put it on video.

Afterward, I took Bob and the boys on to the new "Big Wheeler" in town! The food wasn't too bad. I made a German chocolate cake, and we had a family party for Bob's birthday. He picked up his African suit, and it looks great.

We just got your postcard with the picture of the banana splits. That was nasty, Mom! Ice cream here made with powdered milk doesn't seem to taste the same as the rich cream and eggs I remember in the States!

We had an exciting night while Bob was away. We nearly flooded out! Dal Washer came and put a hole in the back wall to let the water out! The next night it rained and went in the front! Our landlord worked all weekend to remedy some of the problems. He built the driveway up and put another hole in the back wall. The generator was completely underwater, but Bob thinks he can fix it.

I made it to class at the end of the week, but that's about it. I just keep up around here, and that's with help! I need to finish getting ready for tonight. Bob and the boys are home from their bike ride.

Love,

Shirley

October 17, 1983

Dear Mom,

The days are getting much warmer here. We started the air conditioner last night in our bedroom.

John has been sick since last Thursday. He spikes a high temperature at night. He said he had a headache at first. Bob started treating him for malaria on Saturday, but we are still up each night. As soon as Bob comes back from class this morning, we will take him for a blood test and identify his problem.

I didn't go to language class all last week. I've been worn out trying to keep up the house and take care of John at night. Bob got up last night, and I slept in yesterday so am feeling better again.

Bob's office is finally taking shape. We moved out books from two shelves—the hallway and boys' room. We needed to get Matt's bed down from the three-beds-high arrangement. It is just too hot up there.

I finally got the laundry room cleaned out. Some of the canned goods are already rusting, so I'll need to do that on a more routine basis. I made curtains to go over the shelves. We also have Dal Washer's freezer now, so we can cook and bake ahead.

We tried a no-snack week at school, but the heat just wipes Josh out. He needs something! Have to wait for the teachers' verdict, but perhaps each mother can better meet their kids' needs than having the school provide snacks.

The painters came again last week to finish the inside of the outside rooms and garage. So all of the boxes and barrels went to the front porch again. And then, did we get a rain pour! This time Bob was home to keep sweeping, so it didn't flood the living room. I spent all Saturday morning cleaning up, and Bob and the boys began digging ditches after they came home from Kpodzi (Saturday from 9 a.m. to 3 p.m. are workdays for the chapel construction there).

Poor Bob left before dawn on Saturday to get the dump truck from the hospital and got stopped and searched two times before he got there. Checkpoints are routine and good for the country's security, but they sure can be a hassle.

We took a late afternoon drive yesterday. Drove up the mountain to the castle. It is beautiful there—straight from a fairy tale book! We stopped at a little restaurant coming back for a pop and jelly sandwich of sorts.

Love,

Shirley

November 1, 1983

Dear Mom,

I'm not too sure where my time goes here. I have to rest more with the heat, but it still seems like I can't get to all I'd like!

My language teacher Mr. Dzagli is coming to the house for me these two weeks. John just plays here then. It has worked out very well.

Last Saturday was a real blessing to Bob. The national in charge of construction at the hospital came with all his men to make blocks at the Kpodzi chapel! They accomplished so much there. Saturday, for me, was a disaster. I just wasn't functioning. I made pumpkin cookies, and we all went to Andersons in the afternoon for a family party. They showed a videotape, and the kids dunked for apples.

Oh, I finally finished the cushions on that extra chair too. They don't look very professional, but they beat having nothing. My sewing machine is working great. As for my skills. . . .

The last couple of days I've spent in prayer for the missionary kids here. I'm so concerned about their attitudes and comments to one another. Instead of being happy for each other, I hear, "You can't . . . " or "I got this and you don't" or "That's not fair . . . ." My Sunday afternoon group of little people are headed in the wrong direction in this area. John, especially, seems to be picking it up.

I've also been praying about God's will for me. I can't keep up with the routine, and I need or feel the need to have more support from Bob. But if my physical weakness causes him to pull back in areas that brought us here, we may as well be home! I know Satan has won in my attitude at times, so please pray that we all be sensitive to God's leading in all areas so we can find the balance in life here. When I begin to wonder why God has us here, the boys sense it quickly!

The work here is slow, too, Mom. The follow-up is just hard work— Scripture calls it labor! Adzovi will begin a Bible study on Wednesday night this week with a young girl who accepted Christ. The women in Togo are hard and very resistant to the gospel.

It's now 9 p.m. We miss you and love you!

Love,

Shirley

November 8, 1983

Dear Mom,

On Sunday, we went to Kpodzi. Church attendance numbers are down, but we can work with those who come to church. The kids were much easier to handle. It is good to see those who are serious about their decisions for Christ growing in the Word.

Adzovi, along with another missionary lady, had three ladies make decisions for Christ at a pre-prayer service Bible study. Only one of those girls came back. Decisions are quick to be made but living a Christian life here is often done with much persecution. K---, A---, and K--- were beaten in front of their school after standing for Christ. One prayed, and they sang hymns during it all. The school expelled them. So pray for "Shadrach, Meshach, and Abednego"! There is much discussion about their testimony among fellow students.

I have prayed more specifically each morning that the Lord would control the flow through our house and bring those He knows need our ministry. My attitude has changed a lot, and I know when I am joyfully willing, He will do the rest. I've been feeling better, and that helps too.

The boys are just getting home from school, so I'll take another break. It is hot!

Love,

Shirley

November 18, 1983

Dear Mom,

In the last couple of days, we have had our share of casualties! John slipped on the wet porch and hit his head. He also cut his cheek on our slate sidewalk. Bob fixed his cheek with butterfly bandages after he cleaned out some rock pieces with a needle. That same morning, Jim Livingston was part of an accident with a motorbike and pedestrian. They came here for a minor fix-up, and the one girl ended up at the hospital with whiplash. Bob checked today, and she will go home tomorrow.

John has a nasty heat rash on his arm. Josh is doing better with the rash on his head. We got soap and powder from the pharmacy that Salome suggested. Some tiny bugs got on my legs Sunday at church and bit me up bad. "Ants in your pants" here is no joke!

Today Luke hurt his wrist. He was swinging, and the top hook just snapped. Bob was just on his way to the hospital for work, but we caught him. We took Luke to Agou. (It's a German hospital and a half-hour drive from us.) They did an x-ray on his wrist. Sure enough, it's broken. The break is in his right arm, so that is good, as he is left-handed. They put a partial cast to his elbow that can come off in three weeks. It is getting hot here, so three weeks will be plenty long. I gave him one of my pain pills before we left and will repeat it tonight. He has studied for his tests and says he is going to school tomorrow.

Oh, all the boys did super on their report cards! They got all *A*'s and *B*'s. Joshua got a *C*+ in reading, and that was his lowest grade. They study hard, and it is special to get good grades to reward the effort. Josh got an *A* in spelling! With lots of time, he can get it from head to paper now.

The boys have November 24 and 25 off for Thanksgiving. Martha asked us to go to their place for dinner, and then I think we will go to Nigeria. We'll go Christmas shopping and look at the people in Benin who live in houses put up on poles in the water. Uncle Dave is going along to watch the boys at a hotel while we shop. It will be a long trip, but a nice change for us all.

We are having a potluck dinner on Sunday for all of the Kpodzi people. I'm not sure any of them understood what a potluck dinner is, so I invited some to come on Saturday and make up a large pot of chicken-tomato sauce. I'll do a big pot of rice on Sunday. It is also Adzovi's birthday, so we'll make a cake for her, too.

Did I tell you about Bob doing a C-section on the Washer's dog? The dog died, but they wanted to see if they could save the puppies. The dog had seven pups, and now Ann is down to just one. Only time will tell if that last one makes it; although, the puppy seems to be doing well.

Mail is very slow, and I understand it may slow down with the holidays. Think I'll have Bob try to call from Lomé tomorrow again. We have gotten just one letter in the last month, and it was over a month old!

I'm out of paper. Until next time.

Love,

Shirley

November 17, 1983

Dear Mom,

At last, we are getting mail again. Bob brought the mail in, and my 9 p.m. "start writing time" has become 10:50 p.m. because of all the letters we received (Of course, I could not wait to read them later!) Boy, did we hit the jackpot in mail! Praise the Lord! They are letters from the first of September, for the most part.

Luke is doing great with his broken arm. He hardly complains at all anymore. The heat makes him sweat and then itch more, but he has been a good sport.

Our Kpodzi potluck came out so lovely. The Christian nationals all brought a dish to pass, and we even liked most of it! Adzovi was so surprised with her birthday cake. I decorated a three-tier, heart-shaped cake with roses.

We're all doing fine. I've had a couple of good weeks.

Love,

Shirley

November 23, 1983

5:30 a.m.

Dear Mom,

It is a beautiful morning here. The sun is just beginning to show its face. Because we are so close to the equator, there will be full sunlight fast. There isn't much of a dawn or dusk here.

Kofi comes at 6 a.m. to start the wash now. It gets so hot by midday. I like to have the clothes off the line by noon.

Today is full. I need to get us ready for our trip to see the boat people, which will be after our Thanksgiving gathering, which I also need to prepare for today! Martha is coming to watch me do dressing for the turkey! Sure hope you are praying because Andersons put a small fortune into a couple of turkeys and then asked me to fix them! Out here, the turkeys can be tough as nails, so cooking them is a very delicate process. She also asked me to do pumpkin pies, and Luke wants a blueberry pie.

I can't remember if I've shared with you about the bad attitudes the missionary kids were having out here. Prayer changes things, and all the boys are doing so much better. Luke, especially, has recognized how he was catching some bitterness and sharpness. He realized that allowing it to be part of his life would only cause more pain. Praise the Lord. I hope to see more changes soon.

Bob has been trying to make more time to have fun and do things with all the boys. He and John made a tent yesterday, which has become "John's office." John came in and told me he needs a fan for his office too.

Mrs. Dzagli and Adzovi are learning how to knit. It is fun to teach them skills they can use. Adzovi also cut out her birthday dress yesterday, and I'll help her sew it. Bob made me a table in the laundry room for my sewing machine. It works perfectly.

Having an office for Bob has helped us out a lot. He can study, have class, and see medical problems out there. We also got all our medicine, bandages, etc. out and sorted.

Did I tell you John has a large sandbox now?

My health has improved, and I'm not so tired all the time. Guess the iron I'm taking is helping, but God has changed some things, too. I marvel at how He cares for each of us in extraordinary ways as we give ourselves to Him daily. I'm so unworthy of His care and faithfulness. I need to learn more about Him and trust Him in all aspects of my life.

At last count, there were around 28 extra people that came through our house yesterday. I've felt pretty good, so I can handle it right now.

The boys are all up, and Kofi is here starting the wash (we are still using the wringer washer and happy for it).

It has been fun talking to you this morning, and I'll write more later, Lord willing!

Love,

Shirley

November 23, 1983

1:45 p.m.

Dear Mom,

I have 15 minutes before class starts, so I'll update you on my preparations: I made two pumpkin pies, one blueberry pie, two batches of dressing (cornbread and regular giblet), and some fudge for tomorrow. I'll do mashed potatoes and gravy in the morning. I also had one hour of Ewe class during all my preparations, our first Thanksgiving in Togo.

Ellen just came over to get Bob. Seems Nicki, their dog, is very sick! Bob is supposed to know about people and all creatures too. This morning, there were a couple of medical problems, supply needs, and then Mrs. Dzagli came for help with her knitting. Kofi is whitewashing the house. It got dirty with the house flooding, but the drain ditches seem to be doing the job now. We shouldn't have the house-flooding problem anymore.

I drove in Lomé last week! It doesn't sound too fantastic, but you have to see Lomé to appreciate the boldness God gave me. Ha! While in Lomé, Ann and I went shopping and just had fun. We ate lunch at one of the big hotels, and I had a hamburger, fries, pop, and a banana split. It was even sort of American (with a lot of imagination)!

Must go.

Love,

Shirley

November 28, 1983

Dear Mom,

I will not soon forget our first Thanksgiving in Togo. Bob came home late Wednesday night to tell me that his father said Grandpa Porath had passed away on Sunday, and the funeral was on Wednesday. He didn't give any details, and that is still all that I know about it.

We had a big celebration for Thanksgiving. As you might remember from my former letter, I was responsible for cooking the "million-dollar" turkeys that Andersons bought. One can never be too sure about the meat being tender here, so I was a bit apprehensive. Dinner turned out to be delicious, and we all had a great time. The electricity was off in town, but that didn't seem to make any difference as we were all happy to celebrate together, even if there was no electricity for fans!

We got started on our mini-vacation at about 5 p.m. The first night we stayed at the hotel on Lake Togo. We took a boat ride over to Togoville in the morning. After a quick breakfast (a typical French breakfast of bread and hot chocolate), we spent a lot of time getting through customs at the border. It was midafternoon before we headed out to see the boat people in Benin.

Uncle Dave came along with us. He watched the three littlest guys while we went to Lagos. I was sure happy that they hadn't come after the day was over.

Our trip was sad in so many ways. If anyone is being exploited, I think those people are. They live in houses up on sticks and make their living by fishing. We took off fast, hoping to find stores open and things available to buy. There wasn't much at Katanu, so Bob, Luke, and I took off for Lagos, Nigeria. The likes of that day I never want to see again. My heart was heavy, and at the day's end, I thought it would break.

We spent several hours getting through the border. While we were waiting, we witnessed a man getting beat up. It was just like on T.V. but only the real thing! Traveling into Lagos, we were on a double lane freeway, and there was a young girl lying face down, eagle spread, on the pavement beside the inside medium, dead. My stomach was sick all day—even if we had stopped to help, there would have been no way for us to move the body. There was another similar situation while we were in Lagos.

The shops were sparse. There weren't any gifts available for us to buy for Christmas, and the televisions we found there would not work with our video machine. So the day was not worthwhile. We got ready to head back and couldn't find any diesel to fill the truck. We drove for two hours, and at last, a man helped us. We had an opportunity to witness to him and also one other fellow. Pray for them and for the many people who received tracts along the way. Oh, how so many of those people need our Savior and His love!

At this point, I had tried to call you so many times. When the calls went through, there was not an answer at the house. I wonder if you are staying with Grandma or something? Bob said he will have Denny try again tonight on the shortwave to get a hold of you.

I feel so helpless. I wish I could be home right now. I know God answers prayer, and I have certainly been praying for all of you. I will be waiting to hear what happened with Grandpa's death and how Grandma is doing. How are you?

Here are a few other news tidbits before I close: Luke is doing fine with his arm in the cast. He will be thrilled to get it off next week. When we got home yesterday, John had a high temperature and headache. I don't know what he has, but he seems better today.

Josh is writing to his cousin Holly because he wants to get a letter. All of the boys sure do enjoy mail, but they don't get too excited about writing.

I have a massive pile of letters again after our short vacation. For a couple of days last week, we must have received 40 letters! It was nice to know we aren't entirely forgotten. Sometimes I think, "Out of sight, out of mind." And we are definitely out of sight way over here in Togo.

I love you very much. I miss you. My prayers remain with you.

Love,

Shirley

P.S. No place is sacred here. I found ants in the toilet paper last week!

December 5, 1983

Dear Mom,

Bob left for the States in such a rush. I did go out and pick up a few things for you. I hope the pottery makes it home to you!?

Saturday was hectic. Salome came early, and we baked. I had a surprise birthday party for her in the afternoon. In the evening, we went to Ron Washer's home for supper. God is so good—Luke was telling Salome how much she was missing in life because she didn't know what watermelon was! Ann found one, and it was almost like the real thing! God cares and encourages each of us in His unique ways. For us that day, it was a watermelon!

Sunday we ended up going to Kpodzi. John slept through the night with no temperature for the first time all week. I had six extras for dinner. Adzovi came and cleaned up for me. Salome came to check on us and to help me with the little kids for Bible club. The kids made bread dough candle rings. They will be lovely gifts to give their parents for Christmas. The electricity kept going off, but we finished.

Luke is working on language and asked me to help him. His work is already beyond me, but I'm sitting here, giving him moral support. Now Joshua needs to read to me.

It is just so challenging to keep praising the Lord in all things, for we each have a desire to be with those we love right now. Luke and I were talking last night and had to praise the Lord then because we "love deep and are loved" to miss you so much.

Love,

Shirley

December 11, 1983

Dear Mom,

Bob is still in the U.S., but not for VACATION! He needed to make an emergency trip to help get off another container and clear up all the loose ends at the warehouse.

We sure miss Bob. I hope he takes a little time to enjoy being home for all of us.

The boys and I are doing fine with just one major problem last week—the termites were trying to get smart on Bob's books! They ate through the cement to Bob's office and then on to his books. Oh, they are ugly little creatures! Kofi and I got them out. I think! (And hope!)

Bob took home all of the pictures[4] we have taken out here, and I hope he found the time to get prints and send them off to you. I won't hold my breath as he has a lot to do in a short amount of time.

As badly as I would like to see everyone during this particular holiday season, I rest content to be here where the Lord has put us. We count it a special privilege to serve God here in Togo. This morning our purpose in being here was so evident. There was a big fête in the village of Kpodzi (a party in memory of someone who died).

Some of the national Christians warned us that there would be a big fête and perhaps we should change our church time. Pastor Paul said no. When we arrived, my heart was so burdened by the activities of the people. They have no hope without Christ! Please pray with us that God would give wisdom and strength and that His Word will grip the hearts of the people in Kpodzi. This season may they understand the real meaning of Christmas and make it real in their lives!

All the boys are up from naps. Must close. You remain in our prayers.

Love,

Shirley

December 18, 1983

Dear Mom,

I missed Bob so much while he was gone and looked forward to seeing him come home to us. I thought I would be the one to meet him at the airport, but the parents of the Livingstons come earlier that day. So the Livingstons will pick Bob up at 7 p.m. when his flight comes in.

I just have to marvel at how God has taken care of us in Bob's absence. Everyone has been so kind. From little to big things, God has supplied our needs through His people.

Kofi was so good to help me all week while Adzovi was gone helping her sick family. He even came yesterday and mopped the floors and cleaned up the kitchen. I kept up with language study until Wednesday and then canceled my classes for the rest of the week. My head and ears filled up Thursday evening, so yesterday, I slept and stayed in bed. Today is better but still lots of pressure in my ears and neck. It feels like mumps. God has been so close to us and shown us His love so often these past weeks. His grace is sufficient, especially in my weaknesses!

Oh, we have added a new pet. The chameleon came Friday afternoon and is fascinating to watch.

Mom, your card and note have been a real encouragement to me. It is so true that our sacrifice is nothing in comparison to Christ on the cross! I reminded myself of that often these past few days when the desire to be home seemed too strong to rejoice. God is good to give comfort and peace. He has reassured me of His desire for us to be here. And now I can praise the Lord for it, too.

Ann asked me to make a birthday cake for Jesus for our all Togo Christmas carolers and kids' program next Saturday. We drew names to exchange gifts, too. I think I'll make a three-tiered, heart-shaped cake and write, "Let every heart prepare Him room." I've made many cakes (different shaped cake pans and decorations would be very useful here). Unique cakes just make celebrations special! And practice makes perfect. (I'm not so good yet, but my homemaking skills are improving as time passes.) I have many opportunities to practice!

I listened to an audiotape this afternoon on why the Christian suffers (trials, physical pain, etc.). The teacher used a lot from Paul's epistles. Oh, how I desire to let the Lord use me and work through me to be an encouragement to others! I need to be consistent and faithful to Christ daily, even now, in my struggles.

Today I used the words of Paul in Colossians to pray for you:

> For this reason also, since the day we heard about it, have not ceased praying for you and asking that you may be filled with the knowledge of His will in all spiritual wisdom and understanding, so that you will walk in a manner worthy of the Lord, to please Him in all respects, bearing fruit in every good work and increasing in the knowledge of God; strengthened with all

power, according to His glorious might, for the attaining of all perseverance and patience; joyously giving thanks to the Father, who has qualified us to share in the inheritance of the saints in light. (Colossians 1:9-12)

I prayed it for myself, too. I want to be a meaningful prayer warrior and so often don't know where to start. What better way than to pray Scripture!

Love,

Shirley

P.S. Bob didn't make it last night but is in Abidjan (off the coast of Côte d'Ivoire in West Africa). But, we have his suitcases! WAWA! West Africa Wins Again! We just got a card sent to the Boonstra family on December 7, 1982! Almost a year late! I try to answer all the letters we get. (And possibly, seeing that we just got a letter from a year ago, or rather, we got a letter meant for the Boonstra family, we don't get all the letters sent to us, either.)

December 23, 1983

Dear Mom,

It is hard to believe that Christmas is upon us! Instead of getting colder, it's gradually getting warmer as we head into the dry season. We sure won't be skiing and ice skating this winter!

As we pause to consider the most incredible love story ever told—God's son coming to earth—what a privilege to be able to share the Christmas story here in Togo. How thrilling to listen to the new Christians (only making decisions a few months ago) sing many of our favorite Christmas songs in Ewe.

Love,

Shirley

December 28, 1983

Dear Mom,

I trust that your Christmas was special this year. God gave us a lovely time celebrating the birth of our wonderful Savior. The week flew by, and Christmas was here and gone before I spent much time reflecting on being away from home. Just having Bob return from the States made the boys happy.

I relaxed this week. I took all the Christmas decorations down and had the girls clean yesterday. I sewed and finished a sundress for Salmone this afternoon. The dress is for her birthday.

We are headed north at the end of the week to a game reserve here in Togo. It is about a six-hour drive, but it will be worth it for the boys. We are eager to see the large animals that live there! We took the boys last week to Lomé and spent time at the ocean and pool. Bob took them yesterday to the hospital to ride their bikes. Then, to my surprise, they brought their motorbikes back here. They are having a ball against my motherly judgment.

After several Sundays without any salvation decisions at Kpodzi, we had four young men accept Christ as Savior last week. We had our hands full with too many kids, also. When we do a craft of any kind, the kids come from everywhere. I have had to think through our priorities because I stand at the door and keep kids out! Doesn't sound like good behavior for a missionary, does it?

Our weather has been beautiful. It is lovely during the day and almost cold at night. The dry and dusty harmattan is here and getting heavier.

We had our first big football (a.k.a. soccer) game with the churches last Saturday. Our team at Kpodzi lost, but they sure had a good time trying. I think it was good for those young guys just to have jolly fun together. Bob worked at the church all morning, so we were there most of the day. Then, at home that evening, after we got everyone taken care of with some minor surgeries, we locked the doors, turned off the outside lights, and had our family Christmas. Matt read the Christmas story from Scripture this year. He was so pleased with himself.

Sunday night, I talked with the kids about God's many gifts to us in His creation. Togo is a beautiful country. I especially enjoy looking at the many different trees and noting how graceful each one appears. I have been reading in Psalms. How true it is that God is evident in all creation!

I can't think of any more news. I feel especially healthy right now and praise the Lord for that while the boys are off school.

Oh, the chameleon escaped last week while the boys were hunting food for the thing. It was a fascinating pet to watch and also probably one of the ugliest we've had so far!

Love,

Shirley

P.S. Mom, many holidays are coming up in Togo, and often the mail is stopped. Don't be alarmed if you don't get our letters for a while.

January 14, 1984

Dear Mom,

This is an S.O.S. for prayer. We are at the construction stage of designing our home at the hospital. The plans are dependent on how the land lays, available materials, and also the many people involved. It will take unlimited grace to have everyone at peace. Anderson's house is going up now, and we are in the process of designing the inside of ours. (Uncle Dave gave us the outside dimensions to work with and said it has to be three levels because of the slope and roofing materials.)

We need to consider airflow (for when there is no electricity), roof overhang, etc. The list goes on and on and on!

I went with Adzovi to the village last week. During our door-to-door visits, she used Scripture I'd learned in Ewe, and it was such an encouragement to understand more! Even if it is still very little!

We went on a picnic with the Washers yesterday. They forgot the plates and silverware, so it will always be memorable. We were at the hospital, so Guardian and Mama, who watch over the hospital, loaned us theirs—Togo style! (This means we had one large bowl for everyone to eat out of with their fingers.) The kids had a ball.

Matt and Josh went with Kofi today to his village. They were so excited and will be beat when they get home, I'm sure.

The boys were given another bird and a hedgehog this week!

Love,

Shirley

January 16, 1984

Dear Mom,

Bob and I spent yesterday in a fun way. We took the boys out to eat at the local restaurant and then went over to Jim and Ellen's to work on our house plans. We have to stay within specific dimensions as well as shape, so it continues to be a real challenge. We need the house to work for our family and all the diverse hospitality we encounter.

Peggy came to the house about 1 a.m. saying she needed help because one of the blind students was convulsing. They ended up going to Lomé to get medical treatment for him and didn't return until about noon today. The little boy stayed in Lomé for observation. He has many problems, including a shunt that may be blocked. I took all of Bob's classes today so he could rest.

Ewe classes continue to be a challenge for both of us. Bob has about 25 hours a week, and I strive for half of that if possible. But we need to continue so we can accomplish our language hours by the end of our first year in Togo. The boys have also begun to take classes two hours a week. Pray for each of us that we would faithfully study this language so that we can share Christ's love in our new adopted country without being culturally offensive.

Oh, the dog ate the bird again, and the dog let the hedgehog out of the cage, too. That dog knows how to keep all of the attention.

I must keep pecking away at my writing.

Mail is very slow . . . . None lately.

Love,

Shirley

January 17, 1984

Hi, Mom,

Life continues to fly by here at a fast pace. Boy, was I delusional when I thought life would settle down! Bob and I keep busy learning Ewe, keeping up the house we are living in, planning for the hospital house that will be built soon, and taking care of the church work at Kpodzi, too. The chapel building in Kpodzi is coming along. The fellows put a halt on the thatch roof and want to save their money for a real roof. We will just wait until they can save enough. The Chief said we could keep meeting in his compound and office.

Adzovi and I went calling yesterday. This is the highlight of my week now. I am beginning to understand some of the Scripture she uses, and a few simple commands like "sit down!" Ha. The old grandma we always visit was sick yesterday. She has shown much interest in listening to the Word of God, but she hasn't made a decision for Christ.

It is still the harmattan season, and we have lots of dust in the air. It is also hot, and it isn't supposed to be yet! I have my washer running again, and my clothes dry so much faster. Kofi sits with the washer, turns the timer, and fills it with a pail of water for each cycle.

The boys got report cards last week. Joshua had two outstandings on his effort and cooperation. Matt got a perfect 100% certificate for all of his spelling tests, and Luke got the same for science. I guess you could say the boys have adjusted well to school and are getting an outstanding education. They all have to study hard to do well, but they seem willing.

Bob and I are taking this afternoon and overnight to go to Lomé. We have so many errands to do for everybody, but it will still be an excellent time to get away. There is a new steak house in Lomé, and they even serve baked potatoes! We will also look for tile and things for the house at the hospital. There has been a lot of talk, and soon we will have to give them our final plans. Please keep praying that our co-laborers in Christ would keep their perspectives and relationships open and that we would not let houses come between us. As always, there is a big difference in what we would all like to see done with them. The Anderson's home is going up now, and the single missionary ladies plan to move to their house at the end of the month.

Oh, we need carpenters. If you know anyone, send them quickly!

Love,

Shirley

February 9, 1984

Dear Mom,

I have a little while before we send a runner off to Lomé this afternoon. I want everyone to know that we are alive and well. As usual, this week has been full to overflowing.

Besides all of the regular weekly activities, I'll give you a quick fill-in-the-space rundown.

Saturday evening, we had Mr. Kwassi and his family over for dinner. It went so well, and it was a good start to a blooming relationship. It gave me the confidence to start having all of the other people whom Bob would like to invite into our home. All of them are medical, local people: the director of the hospital here in Kpalimé, the doctors at Agou (where we had Luke's arm set), officials in town who Bob has to work with in regards to the hospital, etc. I have been hesitant because I wasn't too sure if I could do a decent African meal! But all went well.

The container, which Bob arranged when he was in the States, came late Monday afternoon! Mom, the piano is beautiful, and everyone is enjoying it. You were all so kind in what you sent. Thank you so much! I can't believe all the goodies you sent too! My freezer filled right up with chocolate chips, nuts, and candies! All of the other gifts that you sent are in a box and ready as the occasion arises.

Kofi decided to burn the trash, even though it is dry and windy. Needless to say, we fought a big fire all afternoon. It turned out to be an excellent way to meet all of the people who live in the village behind us. They had to come out in force to save their village! At least it seemed that way to me.

Last night there was a beautiful sight up the mountain. It was on fire! It looked like a giant, lit Christmas tree. It was like being in Michigan during winter with the snow falling, but it wasn't snow! It was bits of black ash falling everywhere, just like snow! The crackle of fire reminded me of a cozy fireplace, but a drip of sweat off the end of my nose quickly brought me back to reality. I am not in Michigan. I am in Togo. We are in the middle of harmattan season, and daily our surroundings get drier. Fires are everywhere, and I'm reminded that it is God who daily watches over and protects us. Psalm 91:1 says, "One who dwells in the shelter of the Most High Will lodge in the shadow of the Almighty."

I must close and get a couple more letters typed so I can send them in 20 minutes.

Love,

Shirley

February 15, 1984

And the peace of God, which surpasses all comprehension, will guard your hearts and minds in Christ Jesus. Philippians 4:7

Dear Mom,

Isn't God so good to put us where we enjoy being in His service? How fortunate we feel to be in Togo, where God has called us. I reflect upon God's greatness and the fact that He has in His mind a plan for each of us. It is beyond my understanding. Often I feel so unworthy of His care and love for me.

Saturday was a relaxed day. Instead of the usual baking and cooking, I read and did a general fix-up job on myself for the evening. Salome couldn't come, so I was all by myself with the boys. They spent the day playing all of our new musical instruments. Matt is good with the accordion, Luke the piano, and Josh the mouth organ. They each start lessons on Thursday.

That evening, our single co-laborers expressed their love in Christ to the married co-workers by doing a Valentine's banquet! It was such a labor of love: water pool, arch, candlelit table with all the decorations and heart candies (to make it American). They even had things planned for the children. We have a super bunch of single missionaries out here, and our lives would be incomplete without them.

I learned the word for "thief" in Ewe this morning during prayer time. A thief broke into Ron Washer's home last night, and it was real drama. Nobody got hurt, but the thief got away without his clothes or anything else! Thieves here strip down so that you can't grab their clothing.

There are days when I wonder where the time has gone, but when I write our activities down and realize that they are sandwiched in between all of the usual church activities and daily living here, I know where the time goes! The church at Kpodzi is doing well, language study continues along, and school for the boys is coming great!

There is much to think about and be responsible for at Kpodzi. The topic of polygamy came up tonight, and it is a real problem here. It will be the topic of discussion next week. Oh, how we need God's wisdom and guidance in so many areas.

John stepped on a snake this afternoon. It did not bite him, but it scared him. It is so dry that all the creatures are coming out of the jungle for water. The fires continue all around too. God is good to protect us in so many areas.

Love,

Shirley

P.S. It is 11 p.m., and Bob just took his fifth bath of the day. It is hot!

February 18, 1984

Dear Mom,

Greetings from Togo, West Africa!

(Forgive my impersonal tone, Mom. I have many correspondences to catch up on, so I thought I'd give it a go all-in-one with this typewriter function.)

Luke raced home from school yesterday because they had found a snake in the schoolyard. Off he went yelling, *"Coupe, Coupe!"* His machete was in his hand and BB gun, too. That poor snake didn't know that it was up against the Cropsey tribe!

We live in a lovely house with running water (most of the time) and electricity (for 12 hours each day). Our home is cement, has three bedrooms, and an unattached *magasin* (storage rooms and Bob's office). We have a large, walled yard as do all of the houses out here. That was hard for me to get used to at first but have since seen the wisdom in it! All of the doors have locks with keys inside and out. That was another situation to cope with here. It is much better now that the keys are all organized and hanging on marked nails. Our bad habit of not putting things away after we use them became very apparent in the constant case of the "missing key." We will stay in this "in-between" house until our house at the hospital site is built.

The boys are enjoying piano, accordion, and mouth organ lessons. They each started last week and are paying for half of the lessons out of their allowance! (We pay the other half.) This financial commitment should help us all stay faithful to practice time. How we praise the Lord for giving us far more in these instruments than we could have afforded. Isn't God good?

The national Christians here are so warm and gracious to us. They have been a lot of help in teaching us how to be a part of the different ministries without being culturally offensive. We can see this time of preparation here in Kpalimé will be a great asset to us when we move to the hospital site and as we continue to minister in Kpodzi. I praise the Lord that at last the boys are feeling more at home with the children in Kpodzi. It has been a source of concern for me because the national children often displayed their curiosity by pinching, pulling hair, or hitting. The boys found it challenging to enjoy church at all.

These things may sound trivial, but they are signs of adjustment in our human aspect of life. We are just your average family. I'm happy to report we're all saved by grace and living in His power. Because of the unique culture we live in, we face different struggles in this earthly journey. It is always fun to sit back and marvel at how God will work out each of the situations that distract us from fellowship with Him. These distractions can strengthen us in our walk if we allow God to take hold. Or, they can keep us away from our source of life and strength: God, our maker.

Keep praying that my mind would be kept at perfect peace. There are many opportunities to be anything but at peace with yourself or the surroundings out here. Pray for unity among the missionaries. With so many people from so many different backgrounds gathered together in one place and all under extreme pressure, it's easy to rub one another the wrong way, which leads to friction and divisions. We need to function as one body, just as your church body does in the States.

It is with joy that we serve the Lord in the land of Togo. We are building relationships that will give us opportunities to share the most beautiful message of the gospel. Our outreach starts at home with family, neighbors, and friends and then goes out to the many professional and business people who are presently not a part of the outreach ministries in a specific way. It has been a joy to have several of these people in our home. Please pray for this particular ministry and the burden God has laid on our hearts.

Love,

Shirley

February 28, 1984

Dear Mom,

This week has been terrific! I started out feeling so helpless and defeated.

It is hot!

Classes didn't go well last week.

John demanded lots of attention.

There are lots of decisions being made at the hospital that affect us, and a teammate has stopped showing up to prayer meetings.

But I prepared myself for the prayer meeting, and the kids were cooperative. God's Word was shared. I learned another Bible verse in Ewe and made some village calls. Josh and I worked out his homework (with lots of tears!), and he said his verse. He got a *B-* and an *A* in spelling! God very plainly has been my Helper. (Marked with a capital *H* because I needed God's help!)

Bob is a traveling student. He just can't get any uninterrupted study time at the house. Since we're determined to make language a priority for him, "other things" must go for a time. Also, because Bob wasn't here, my language class was interrupted four times in 45 minutes this morning! Please pray for wisdom in this area.

Love,

Shirley

March 6, 1984

Dear Mom,

I heard that my dear foster sister, Faith, has gone home to be with Jesus. After receiving word, Joshua said, "Mom, we have to go home. Everybody is dying!" How I long to be with family and friends during these difficult and sad times—to comfort and receive comfort! God has given me peace as I wait upon Him. His grace is all-sufficient. Josh is also still trying to go home; pray that God's peace will quiet his heart. This is our promise:

> For You do not delight in sacrifice, otherwise I would give it;

You are not pleased with burnt offering.

The sacrifices of God are a broken spirit;

A broken and a contrite heart, O God, You will not despise.

(Psalm 51:16-17)

God has been very much alive in the ministries here, and we praise Him for all that we see Him doing. However, that often raises opposition from Satan. Since accepting Christ, the Chief has faced many difficult and sad circumstances. Our lives have not been without attack, either. How we must praise the Lord for giving and re-giving the assurance that we are in His will and abiding in His love. We need your prayers that our attitudes and motives would remain right before God and man always.

My health continues to improve but at a plodding pace. I praise the Lord for all that He allows me to do and don't want to overstep my boundaries in this area. It doesn't pay in the long run, right?

Bob struggles to get in his language hours. We can see that it will take us a long time to be fluent in this tonal language. As we remain faithful to the task, we know that God will do the rest. Slowly and steadily, we will continue to get the language hours done for this year.

It is late, but I wanted to get a short note off just so that your prayers would be better directed on our behalf. Thanks for listening.

Love,

Shirley

March 15, 1984

Dear Mom,

God has been so close to me in the last couple of weeks. He has given such a sweet peace to me. I've been able to control my thoughts of "maybe" someone is upset with me. I've done it by memorizing more Scripture! There is no time for self-pity or otherwise. Luke and I are going to try, with God's help, to learn James. He already does a lot for school, but memorization comes easy for him.

It has started to rain more, and my head burns again.

John was busy this week. He spent the night with Kofi last night! During the day, his friend Yaovi came to play. I can see he's ready for school.

The electricity hasn't come on yet, and it is hot!

Bob made a "hut call" last night. The Chief's uncle is in bad congestive heart failure. Pray for our little village.

We are spring cleaning now that the harmattan season has cleared. It was so lovely to see the blue sky and clouds again. The mountain is in view, too. Because it has been so dry, I can see from our backyard a small village in the middle of a palm grove.

Oh, we had three men from a Bible organization come yesterday. One was the president of the Bank of Ghana and the other a businessman. The third man is the president of the Bible organization in Lomé.

He says they will start printing Bibles in Ewe next year!

Love,

Shirley

April 1984 Newsletter

Dear Mom,

God's hand at work is very evident here, but so is the opposition.

In the last two months, the brother (age 40) and sister (age 62) of the Chief of Kpodzi have died. Pray that despite this, and the many other difficult circumstances he faces, his walk with the Lord will be strengthened.

As the hot, dry season draws to a close, we thank God for giving us strength and health as we share the Lord Jesus and continue in language study. We are counting the days until we officially have our "one-year of language study" done in Togo.

Driving home from church, John said, "It feels like it rained on me all morning." He looked like it! He was wringing wet with sweat!

We thank you for your faithful prayers. We know if much is to be accomplished for God in Togo, much prayer is also needed.

Love,

Shirley

P.S. Soccer match results: Kpodzi 2, Kpalimé 3!

April 2, 1984

Dear Mom,

Greetings from sunny, hot, humid Togo!

The air is so heavy today that it will be a close tie between a good shower and my clothes getting dry. The people are getting their crops planted, and we very much need rain. My clothes will dry eventually!

At our last school committee meeting, we voted to continue renting the buildings where our school is currently located. Please pray for us to fill school positions with short-term teachers. We have two interested short-term teachers. One lady is working on getting financial support to come at the start of the new year, and another possible teacher is in the praying stages. Our elementary students will double in number next year, and I may need to help at the school. That will make it impossible for me to teach John kindergarten. God has it all planned out, and we just each need to be sensitive to His leading in our lives.

I spent another long day with one of the other fellow workers last week. She needs to get a lot of things settled with the Lord. Interpersonal relationships are such an immense strain on us out here. If it were just missionary work, all would be great, but I also know that would have disadvantages: to be alone in the work.

Kids are just out of Ewe class now. My peace is gone! John was such a doll today. He just played and let me rest. The boys are all fine. The school is going out to the Blind Center tomorrow afternoon for a spring break day. No snow days make for a long year!

The red ants are around in force, and it is time to spring clean. Better close. You can tell that I don't have much news.

Love,

Shirley

April 14, 1984

Dear Mom,

I have enjoyed your letters of encouragement so much. Thank you for being so faithful to write to us. I know it takes precious time, but it means so much to me.

Matt broke his back in two places! The kids were playing tag. Matt ran on top of the seven-foot cement wall around our house and jumped onto the carport. The carport has a bamboo frame with palm branches for the roof. Packed dirt provided the landing for Matt. When I got to him, he was as white as a ghost! Despite all this, Matt is doing very well and healing from his injury. His teachers come and help him with his schoolwork. It was easier for him to rest before the boys were off for spring break. Now it is hard for him to see the other kids out playing. If he stays down now, it may save him years of back trouble or any complications. Bob hooked up the computer for Matt, and he has been playing lots of games.

I am tired but doing okay. I've gotten myself into bed very early this week and just take things a day at a time.

Mr. D, president of a Bible organization, is here this weekend. Without asking permission first, he asked the whole town to the Kpalimé church this afternoon. We are not sure he is a Christian and have had to take a stand for separation. It is a sticky situation. Pray! He has undoubtedly supplied lots of Bibles and opened up opportunities to witness to people, but we are uneasy. Pray that God's message of salvation is not muddled for the people we have been working with.

There isn't any flour to be found, so meals are more of a challenge. Must go and start supper.

Love,

Shirley

April 15, 1984

Hi, Mom,

It is a warm day with a lovely breeze here. The sky is so clear, and it is a beautiful blue color. The bush is green and lush again after the recent rains. It's an artistic picture to display the radiant creation of our Lord to one and all who will just look. This is truly a country overflowing with God's handiwork. I wish you could see it.

As I come to the close of another year, I reflect on all that God has done in my life. (Birthdays do have a way of making you reflect!) How I thank God for the lessons He teaches me, for His patience in my life, and His faithfulness to me. What a privilege to be here in the country of Togo! He stretches us to the limit at times and always encourages and strengthens us in our weaknesses.

Salome made me a beautiful birthday cake and also planned a surprise party for me yesterday. Since I gave her my limited knowledge of decorating cakes, it has been a joy to watch her make others happy by creating cakes for them. To have her do it for me was a real thrill. (I also taught her count cross-stitch this afternoon!)

We fed 12 extra at the table this noon and five extra tonight. I praise the Lord for His abundant provision in our lives! It makes it possible to feed and keep feeding everyone who comes to our door! Some days I think God makes the food multiply, just as He did for the disciples!

Our dog Blackie had three pups. Mother and puppies are all doing just fine, and the boys are delighted.

Matt's back is not hurting anymore, but he is a pill to keep down. It is more challenging with the boys off school and out playing! He just wants to join the fun.

Bob has decided not to take any time off from language. He is trying to get as much done as he can before our hectic summer begins.

Keep praying for MK teachers. It looks like we have two reliable candidates for the job. Both of these ladies will have many needs to be cared for before they arrive here. Kelli Thayer from Calvary Baptist church of Ypsilanti, Michigan, is one of them. Do you remember her?

I started a Bible study in French with Salome last week and will have the same study in Ewe to help Adzovi with the ladies at Kpodzi. I don't know enough of either language, so please pray for us as we seek to teach and guide. God helped me understand the French, and I know He can do the next step too.

It is time to get the boys ready for church tonight. Always enjoy your letters!

Love,

Shirley

April 20, 1984 Newsletter

But we do not want you to be uninformed, brothers and sisters, about those who are asleep, so that you will not grieve as indeed the rest of mankind, who have no hope. For if we believe that Jesus died and rose from the dead, so also God will bring with Him those who have fallen asleep through Jesus. 1 Thessalonians 4:13-14

Dear Mom,

The Chief has had so many sorrows lately. Let me share the story of his most recent tragedy.

Driving down the bumpy, dirt road, I could hear the wails coming from the Chief's compound. Upon arriving, we were greeted by several of the believers and taken in to see the body. A healthy 22-year-old college student lay lifeless on the cement floor. Kumola had come home to help in the fields for a couple of days before the holiday ended. A fire broke out, and he was overcome by smoke in the field.

We went back early the next morning to give our support to the Chief and his daughter, Marie, who is also a believer. Bob spent time with the Chief in his office, and I went with Adzovi to find Marie. When she saw us, she came and brought two chairs, and we sat all day in front of the body, witnessing a very solemn occasion in a culture very different from our own. God has used this experience in my life to make my burden even heavier to reach these lovely people who have no hope without our Lord.

There was competition and confusion between the fetishers[5] and the Catholics all day, along with the mourners. This confirms that we are missing something in our teachings. Christians should walk victoriously through all of life's experiences by having a Spirit-controlled life. Bob was able to have a good service after the gravesite ceremonies. God took control of the crowd and gave peace so that Bob could share from God's Word to encourage our believers as well as share the gospel with those who don't yet believe.

Please pray for us and the Chief.

Love,

Shirley

P.S. Mom, I wanted to add a little more for you, as we are sending this letter out to all our prayer partners. Matthew, with his back broken in two places, is doing well. He doesn't have any complications at this point and is moving all over in his bed. People have been so good to stop and see him. He keeps a visitor book and gives out bubble gum. His teacher has come twice today to have classes with him.

The doc at Agou said it might take two months for Matthew to recover, but Bob thinks he is recovering quicker than expected.

We had planned to go with another family to Lake Togo during the break. However, knowing how temperamental another family is about anything we do, I wasn't sure I was up to the repercussions and had asked God to make His will plain to us. He did (in the form that Matt needs to stay home and rest), and I do thank Him. I realize more and more we can't change our lives to please everyone, but I sure don't want to make trouble for anyone either.

There is a team of 26 people coming out in the middle of May. They will stay at the hospital during the week and then rotate to each of our homes in groups on the weekends. I am not responsible for any of them except on weekends, and I will also help make food to feed them during the week. I will have to start planning now to survive. It is a little harder because I don't like to keep much food around for very long, with the electricity going off so much. It is so hot here.

Take care and know we love and miss you! Since the Andersons are leaving soon for the States, Martha asked the boys what she could bring back for them. One of ours said, "Grandma Shannon!"

April 30, 1984

Greetings from Togo!

I just returned from a morning of calling with Adzovi at Kpodzi. What a thrill it is to sit and listen to the gospel going forth. We shared with three ladies and two gentlemen, along with a group of children who quietly listened. While we were walking out, we stopped to visit an older man who came to church last Sunday. He wants to accept Christ as his Savior. He asked us! We shared some verses with him, and Bob will go back later today. Because of their quick response to the gospel, we need to be very sensitive to the Holy Spirit's leading, not going ahead before God's plan for salvation is understood. I don't speak either language well enough to lead a person to Christ in Ewe or French. Please keep praying for me in this area.

Bob left to go to the mountain to find a quiet place to study this morning. He wants to get at least six hours of uninterrupted study today, which is impossible at our house. But from my experience this morning, you see how crucial it is for us to get the language!

Matthew is going to school for half days this week and doing well. He tires quickly and just isn't up to par after breaking his back three weeks ago. We told him that he couldn't keep up with accordion lessons for the rest of this school year, which was a disappointment.

The hospital is close to being out of money, so we will need to change some construction plans, which was disheartening. That means we are putting all the money into the hospital to finish, and at present, we have no house at the hospital compound. Change seems to be the theme in life out here.

Even the puppies are growing and changing. Someone put a claim on one of the puppies, and that upset Matt, too. *But,* God is so good. My brother sent us videotapes of our family, including my grandparents telling their history and another of just entertainment. The boys just sat and soaked them up.

(Thank you so much for the package you sent to Matt! God got it here just the right day. Matt wouldn't get up or speak to us for about an hour—did I pray! Then your package arrived!)

We had our first church service in the new chapel at Kpodzi last Sunday. There was a threat of rain in the sky all morning, but we didn't get wet—even with a palm leaf roof. (They are waiting to raise funds to have a better roof, so now a palm leaf roof will do.) We did not have the baptismal service, though. Bob spent all last week interviewing the candidates and just didn't feel that most of them were ready. Keep praying for our new believers and their spiritual growth. It makes me more aware of the beautiful, Chrisitan inheritance I received from growing up in a Christian home where I was both taught and shown Christ's love.

Continue to pray for the two MK teachers who are coming to Togo. We still aren't sure what to do with John and his first year of education. There are no other children starting kindergarten next year. The older boys are doing fine, and they have gotten a superb education this year. Everyone is caught up in the areas that they lacked from all of the moving around in French schools.

The rains continue to fall, and the countryside is more green and lush all the time. I'll leave you with this verse to help you imagine all the joy I have from the beauty here. Psalm 19:1 says, "The heavens tell of the glory of God; And their expanse declares the work of His hands."

Love,

Shirley

May 11, 1984

Now He who supplies seed to the sower and bread for food will supply and multiply your seed for sowing and increase the harvest of your righteousness; you will be enriched in everything for all liberality, which through us is producing thanksgiving to God. 2 Corinthians 9:10-11

Dear Mom,

Several of the missionary ladies gathered for prayer time in conjunction with the whole ABWE missionary force praying for worldwide evangelism each first Tuesday of the month. One of the gals shared 2 Corinthians 9:10-11 with us before we started. What an encouragement to realize that God promises to use us as we allow Him to increase our storehouse.

An update on our health: I am beginning to feel better again after having a rough week with the same old, post-encephalitis problems. Matthew is recovering nicely and will be able to increase his activity to light jogging next week, to his delight! (It has been about six weeks since he fell and broke his back in two places.)

Bob is busy trying to get in language hours to officially finish his first year at the end of June. After that time, he hopes to put time in at the hospital again. However, this morning, Bob didn't get any time in as one patient after another came to the house! With all of the trips he has made to Agou hospital lately, they gave him more privileges. So now he can send patients with a slip of what he wants done, and Agou hospital will do it for him. That will save him hours.

Last weekend we had a good time with the kids. Bob challenged them to ride to the top of the little mountain near us. It is about 2,000 feet high. Bob made it except the last quarter mile, which was the steepest. Luke made it all the way to the top! Afterward, we followed a winding, dirt road for about 20 miles until we came out on the mountain's right side near the hospital where the waterfall is located. It was a beautiful drive and so pleasant at that altitude! We also practiced our Ewe and sat with the village people there. My white skin scared more than one of the villagers. It was plain to see they had not seen a white person before!

We have trouble with prowlers again. Sunday morning, the dogs were barking, and Bob caught some guys in the yard. They ran, so we only got a good look at one of them. They showed up in the living room of another missionary later in the morning and were armed. Last night everyone was in Lomé picking up the short-term team, and the dogs would not stop barking. Bob got home around midnight, and while he was showering, I heard someone running along the side of the house. At this moment, Bob is seeing what can be done about all the intruders!

(Oh me! The vacuum sweeper just got plugged into the wrong current! Will have to handle that.)

It looks like Dr. Dave Clutts found some money, and I think they are going ahead with our house on the hospital compound now!? One can't be too sure; nevertheless, we're still here until it is built. This is contrary to what we decided as a medical committee, so I am not sure what is going on.

I just looked on my calendar. I have company coming every day this week!

Love,

Shirley

May 21, 1984

Dear Mom,

It is hot in Togo! We hear that it is trying to warm up in the U.S.A. too! I'm going to defrost the freezer just to have a good snowball fight with the boys.

We are in the middle of two weeks of hosting 25 college-age kids from Florida. Last Saturday evening, we all met at the top of the nearby mountain for a potluck. The scenery was beautiful, and the pond so peaceful that my mind went directly to these verses:

> He lets me lie down in green pastures;
>
> He leads me beside quiet waters.
>
> He restores my soul;
>
> He guides me in the paths of righteousness
>
> For the sake of His name. (Psalm 23:2-3)

The kids formed a choir and sang down by the pond. It was so good to hear their voices raised to heaven, declaring the goodness of our God!

Matt is back to his normal activities after breaking his back several weeks ago. He isn't doing it all with the same enthusiasm, but we praise the Lord for His care in this situation. I rested last week one morning and then did all of my cooking and baking for the team. I was able to keep up with all my language hours, too, so praise the Lord! We're almost at the end of our language year!

We took the three girls staying with us up the mountain the other day. Bob and the boys took them on the walk back to the big waterfall. I have yet to make it all the way but did enjoy another afternoon in that little village. I only scared one little girl yesterday. I sang with the kids, "My God is so Big." Well, it is a start when you can't communicate well!

Each of our national helpers has pitched in and helped so much with the extra people. They are becoming real friends in Christ, and it is such a special feeling. Kofi washed and ironed clothes on Saturday for the girls staying with us. Salome came and fixed an African meal and went calling at Kpodzi with them. Adzovi pounded fufu and worked at making the house look sparkling. All just because they wanted to help! God takes care of each of us in such unexpected ways. He never asks us to do more than He can do through us!

Boys will soon be home for lunch. I have enjoyed our visit.

Love,

Shirley

May 31, 1984

Dear Mom,

During my quiet time this morning, my thoughts floated to 1 Peter 1:15-16. It says, "But like the Holy One who called you, be holy yourselves also in all your behavior; because it is written: 'YOU SHALL BE HOLY, FOR I AM HOLY.'" Isn't it fantastic how we can see God's faithfulness? He brings each new day to us. It is a great comfort to know that we love and serve a Holy God. The choice is ours: to live a holy life means joy for us, so pray for me in this struggle with my inner person as I pray for you. I need more time to meditate upon His Word and a more willing spirit to let it control my life.

Can you believe that we have been in Togo for a year now? How I must daily walk with Him! The challenges have been many as we adjusted, but there has also been a rich harvest of rewards as we've been faithful to what God has given us. The hospital will soon be officially open, and we will move into our new house on the hospital compound. I'm excited to see what God has in store for us as we transition into this new phase.

It is raining this morning. John is off to Kpodzi with Bob. Adzovi is busy with her responsibilities for the day, so I took the opportunity to spend some extended time in prayer and reading. After two hectic weeks with the 25 kids from Pensacola, Florida, I needed the extra time to soak in His many blessings.

Let me share some of the highlights from the past couple of weeks. Our people at Kpodzi prayed together and gave, and we were able to put the roof on the church! We had our first Wednesday night prayer service last week with fantastic attendance. On Sunday, we were the "church on the move." We took the whole church with several vehicles and the large trailer to the river for our first baptismal service. What a blessing to see our first fruits baptized along with our oldest son, Luke. God is so good!

At the same time God was blessing, Satan was busy to discourage. Thieves were breaking into our house! They just ripped the back screen off and ruined the outside doorknob on the back door. Mensa, who lives in the village behind our house, heard the noise. He ran to the Kpalimé church to get help, and they caught one of the men. The men proceeded to beat the captured burglar, which is the custom here. Pray that we will know God's compassion and love and be able to teach it to our brothers in Christ here. Pray that God would continue to give us a spirit of peace in this situation and not of fear.

The kids finished language class last week. I did a treasure hunt in Ewe for them, and we had refreshments to celebrate a job well done. They know the Romans Road in Ewe plus simple sentences and questions, also some songs. The boys are all better able to communicate on an elementary level. What a challenge the tones are for all of us!

It is now 3:30 p.m. The boys are back from school and off to the hospital with Bob to see how the construction is going. Joshua wants to check up on the two pups that have been given away. I have company coming for dinner tonight and also need to do a couple of errands, so I'll close for the time.

What a year it has been!

Love,

Shirley

Part Three: What God Can Do

From 1985 when the hospital opened to 1993 when we said goodbye to Togo, God's work in our lives was evident. As the hospital grew, we leaned on God's wisdom to develop systems and policies that would serve the patients and staff. As our children and the children of other missionary families grew, I looked to God for help to establish a school and facilitate the high school program.

We experienced grief from the deaths of beloved friends, and after years of peace, heartache over Togo's political unrest. We had furloughs back to the States for times of rest and to share all the work God was doing in West Africa —and we had unexpected medical trips to see doctors about my continued health struggle.

Although willing, we often felt inadequate to deal with the huge issues presented to us. However, God continue to open doors for us through the ministry at the hospital, church at Kpodzi, many Bible studies, and opportunities for hospitality and correspondence. Our slogan at HBB was, "We don't believe in miracles, we rely on them." Through it all, we saw what God could do with willing hearts and hands.

June 1, 1985

Dear Mom,

Here we are 12 days before the hospital dedication! As we work heartily as unto the Lord, you pray fervently. We desire to see God receive all the glory for what He has and will accomplish here in Togo.

First, let me tell you about the progress at the hospital.

The hospital grounds look nice. The outpatient clinic is all ready to go, except for the exam tables that are being finished up now. We organized the warehouse down to the last massive stack of shelves. (The most difficult because everything that didn't have a place got put there!) We will have a big work day tomorrow to bring the hospital closer to completion on the inside.

I am coming out of a bad relapse and have spent most of the last month in bed. Just as I began to feel like I might be healed of this illness, it suddenly reappeared! Isaiah 61:3 speaks of giving the "cloak of praise instead of a disheartened spirit," and I can testify that He surely can do that. I must confess to some low moments, but as I turn to Christ, He has given grace.

With the help of Martha Anderson and three teachers that came out with the Pensacola team, John and I finished up his first school year! All the boys did fantastic this year. They worked hard and are happy for the summer break. I was elected chairman of the school committee. So for me, the work begins to prepare for next year. Our teachers have been super, and I am confident of another fantastic year with Kelli here to keep things on track.

In his salutation to the Colossians, we join with Paul that we "have not ceased praying for you" (Colossians 1:9). I prayed for you today!

Love,

Shirley

June 12, 1985

Dear Mom,

The Karolyn Kempton Memorial Christian Hospital in Togo, West Africa, is officially open! Here's what I wrote up for the newspapers and other correspondence:

After an eight-hour tropical downpour, the hot sun dawned over the grove of palm trees. The sun's radiance dried and prepared the Karolyn Kempton Memorial Christian Hospital for its dedication to our Lord.

June 12, 1985, marks the end of many years of planning and preparing. It is the birth of medical surgical evangelism in Togo, West Africa, through outpatient care and a 25-bed hospital facility.

A large tent housed the stage and podium, two large palms on either side of the stage, and several chairs. To the right, many Togo flags waved in the breeze around the circle drive. Before us, the brightly wrapped poles represented the flag colors of Togo and the United States. To my left, through a palm branch arch, a large floral arrangement added beauty to the table of food. To the rear of the tent stood a large bamboo shelter lined with benches to seat most of our visiting guests. The roads carried many traveling feet throughout the morning.

The ceremony began with speeches from many Togo dignitaries. It included comments from Dr. David Clutts, resident surgeon, and Dr. Wendell Kempton, president of the Association of Baptists for World Evangelism (our endorsing mission). The three children of the late Mrs. Karolyn Kempton spoke in memory of their mother. Approximately 1,500 people enjoyed the program. The ribbon-cutting ceremony was a touching moment. One of the missionary children, Becky Anderson, carried the scissors, and Atanti Assanh, a young Togolese girl, presented the bouquet. The Blind Center choir offered many special numbers throughout the morning.

We could hear, "To God be the glory, great things He hath done!" from the male ward where missionaries and tour groups joined in a midafternoon song of praise. Many echoed prayers of dedication. Humbled hearts knelt before the throne of grace and gave credit for the many miracles of days past, reconfirming our faith in all God will accomplish in the days ahead.

We dedicated the hospital to the glory of God. Our goal is to help people with their physical problems and see them come to have a relationship with the Lord Jesus Christ.

Togo television, radio, and newspaper covered this event.

Respectfully submitted,

Shirley Cropsey, Missionary to Togo, West Africa

July 25, 1985

Dear Mom,

The dedication day of the hospital was above all our expectations. THANK YOU for your prayers, for we are very aware that it was only through God that everything was accomplished. The outpatient clinic is now open, too.

The day before the clinic opened, many Togolese slept all night near the clini's doors to be the first ones in. There were about 500 people that first day. Many patients came to see if they could find help for medical problems that no one else could help. Others came to see how we would treat them or what *Hôpital Baptiste Biblique* was all about.

What a grand opportunity to share the gospel with so many folks! We start every day with a missionary staff prayer meeting, then an employee chapel, followed by a patient chapel. One man asked a colleague, "Just when does this eternal life begin, anyway?" For many, the first seeds of the gospel are planted, and we hope as they return again that we can water and nurture that seed to see lives changed for eternity.

The spectrum of disease is immense and very challenging. It includes the following: leprosy, cataracts, intestinal parasites of every size and shape, malnutrition, O.B. and gynecological problems, as well as other rare findings.

The people are so patient. We praise God that they are very open to the gospel!

Love,

Shirley

October 17, 1985

Dear Mom,

This letter is overdue, and as I look at the calendar, it is difficult to know how to begin.

Let's start with the weather. Since I last wrote, harmattan has tried its best to settle in. However, it continues to rain, too! Yes, it is strange weather for Togo. The days are getting hotter, but it is still cooling off nicely at night.

The clinic patient load remains stable with an average of 70 patients in a given day. The hospital is also open. Most patients are critical care types. The O.B. patients are complicated cases. Bob has seen many difficult forceps and C-section deliveries.

Bob is on call 24 hours a day. He is the only doctor on the compound practicing medicine. (Dr. Dave is still working construction.) Bob is worn out, and the kids wonder who daddy is. This is all so new that it will take time to get everything running smoothly. Pray for each of us that we will have wisdom to make changes when needed.

As for school, there is one way to be in tune with your kids' academic victories and defeats, be the teacher! I had the privilege of teaching for the past month and again last week in art. By God's grace, we all survived! Kelli has not been feeling well. Pray for her.

Luke is in 7th grade and has lots of homework. He earns money after school by cutting yards and hauling field stones for Dr. Dave. Matthew is in 5th grade and is finding it to be a significant transition period. Pray for him as he changes his study patterns and develops more independence in his studies. Joshua gives 3rd grade his best effort. He was forced into cursive writing. At least, that's what he would tell you; however, he wrote a letter last night on his own, not printed! John, who is in 1st grade, is more ready for school this year. The things he struggled with last year, he just knows this year!

The school committee has also taken a lot of my time. We are making many decisions: admission policy, high school curriculum, responsibilities, construction of a building, etc. As in most things, the prep time consumes more time than the actual projects!

Togo life continues to keep us entertained through minor incidences: discovering a flat tire on my way to class, getting stopped twice by the police, finding a two-foot spitting cobra that hid under the rug at school, John and Josh crashing on the motorcycle, heavy rains weighing down the overgrown weeds along the road, etc. You'll have to visit to appreciate the scope, but praise the Lord! He has us in His care! I have been reading in 1 Peter 2:9*b* that says, "So that you may proclaim the excellencies of Him who has called you out of darkness into His marvelous light."

That is why we are here, to "proclaim the excellencies." This is a rambling letter, but I hope it gives you a glimpse into life in Togo with the Cropseys.

Love,

Shirley

November 7, 1985

Dear Mom,

We have many praises as well as requests. To let you know what is going on, I will tell you all that God is doing with and through us.

The first is that we have been able to get needed drugs through a Togo pharmacy!

All of our boys have schistosomiasis after swimming in an infected pond of sewer at Bethania. They are all on a very toxic drug and have been sick (nausea, vomiting, headache, eyes hurt, chest pain). Please pray with us for complete recovery! Even with this treatment, there isn't always a cure. This is the fifth day of treatment. Because of the toxicity, Bob is taking them off for two weeks, and then they will take it another five days.

Bob is exhausted and never seems to get ahead of things. We need God's wisdom in knowing how to handle life's demands. Because it is often life and death he deals with at the hospital, it's hard to find the needed rest. There isn't another doctor nearby.

We also need continued protection from the environment around us. (The army ants marched into the house next door last Monday night!) As the weather gets drier, the fires will start up again, and the snakes come out for water. Several weeks ago, a hooded cobra came up on the porch at school. At Luke's cry, it dropped and hid under the rug in the front of the door.

The usual weekly schedule continues. Clinic days are Monday, Wednesday, and Friday, with surgery Tuesday and Thursday. We get at least one urgent visit from Guardian nightly requesting Bob's help. I am keeping up with French language study, a Bible study, and school responsibilities. Our basket weaving went great, and next, we will have the blind students come and teach our kids how to weave stools! That should be great interaction for both groups!

Nice visiting with you.

Love,

Shirley

November 14, 1985

Dear Mom,

It is Thursday morning, and all is well. I just walked back from the hospital, doing errands. Bob is in surgery this morning.

The boys are acting more like usual again. They will still go back on the medicine again in a couple of weeks. Ann Washer said she read in the *Reader's Digest* that there is a new drug out to treat schistosomiasis! If someone could find out about it for us, that would be great.

I spent yesterday morning trying to figure out school matters: money for the new school, personal accounts, and concerns from another parent. This job is a lot of work and entails a lot more than I know how to do efficiently!

We are busy planning Thanksgiving and Christmas activities. We will have the hospital staff to our house for Thanksgiving dinner and our annual Mango bowl. I am supposed to get turkey cookies made for the school party, plus two pies and dinner for Thanksgiving. I hope to start on it today and freeze them, or I'll never get it all done. HELP!

Love,

Shirley

January 8, 1986

Dear Mom,

I spent all afternoon yesterday getting our school books straightened out again. They are a mess! Wrote another long letter to headquarters. That should really confuse them. Ha!

The school is going up. The door frames are in place, and the bricks are almost window-level. It would have been nice to have someone who knows what they are doing design the school instead of us "do-it-yourself" missionaries, but it's getting built!

I went down to the hospital and helped last night. Did a couple of x-rays and got a large sliver out of the throat of a three-year-old boy who fell with a stick. I practiced my French. Don't think I would do well in an emergency, but it was fun to get my hands, as they say, "wet again" in nursing.

I have to start getting my annual report done for next Tuesday. We write goals and how we plan to carry them out for next year. When I saw that request, I thought, SURVIVE, SURVIVE, SURVIVE! I don't believe that is what the leader has in mind, though. (I'm smiling, are you?) Really, I want to thrive! I guess survival is the first step.

Just finished typing questions for the book of Timothy for my Bible study with Mrs. Dzagli. Got any suggestions for our next study?

Love,

Shirley

January 17, 1986

Dear Mom,

We have mail again! It is good to hear from everyone, but my desk is smothered. Sent 200 pieces of mail just last week! That is a small price to pay because we enjoy the encouraging letters from people back home.

Last week we had a lot of sad things happen at the hospital. Bob worked so many hours. The boys and I went often to the hospital to bring him food, and then I would end up nursing. All hands on deck! I enjoy it a lot, but I know I need to learn how to communicate in French a lot better. Here are some things that happened while I was at the hospital.

A little boy about seven years old came into the hospital with tetanus. He wasn't doing too bad. I told him that Jesus loved him and he gave me the most beautiful smile. He died before I came back a day and a half later. That same night, a lady Bob had taken back into surgery, whom Matt watched, died.

The boys have seen such sad things here and have handled it well, but how we need wisdom in how to parent in such extreme situations! I grew up without knowing that there was such poverty and sadness, yet my boys encounter it every day. I thank the Lord for my happy years of growing up and just pray that this, as a different situation, will be a good one for the boys.

Love,

Shirley

February 24, 1986

Greetings from Togo,

In the last month, there have been many changes in the lives and surroundings of the Cropsey home!

The men started on the school floor last Saturday, and we expect that it will take from two to four weeks. The other parts of the school progress at different levels too. The best part is that it is paid for, and the books still balance!

The ministries at the hospital continue to see fruit. Dr. Dave and Dr. Bob take turns staying here for Sundays, and last Sunday, they started a chapel service for the patients and their families caring for them. Several have come to know the Lord through this ministry.

The three Bible study groups in the villages continue. The patient load remains about the same, and Bob continues to take all the night calls. The Lord gives strength and rest when it is most needed! We do not have an administrator for the hospital, nor anyone to be in charge of the continued structural changes and construction, so Bob has taken those responsibilities. But God controls the hearts of those over us! We have permission to hire a Christian man to fill our dismissed pharmacy aide person. The medical committee has committed to hiring only Christians at this point.

Love,

Shirley

P.S. Did I tell you about making the boys' lunch one day when it was still dark? I thought that the honey seemed dark in spots!? The boys came home beside themselves because giant sugar ants were in the sandwiches, and the ants were still moving! I got a detailed description from Ann of how each kid reacted. Luke just pinched his ants out and ate the sandwich. Now that's adjusting!

March 8, 1986

Dear Mom,

We had a lovely family party for Matt's birthday yesterday. I made ice cream, but saltwater got into it. It was a flop! So much time down the drain, oh me. We had fun anyway, and Matt is a year older now.

Did I tell you about the dedication service for the school? We named it Sager Hall after Kurt who has come to Togo so many times to help us with construction. Luke is doing a fantastic job keeping up with the cleaning. With much encouragement, Matt and Josh are doing the yard work satisfactorily.

With the rains getting heavier, the ants are all coming in. There is just about any size and color you could wish for in the house with us. I cleaned out our dresser yesterday looking for a nest because they were in the clothes, but I didn't find the source there. So onward!

Our outside helper, Mensaga, has the whole yard planted into grass now. The Togolese plant a few patches at a time spaced out and let it fill in. Right now, it doesn't look too good. So we wait for it to grow together. Weeds work okay for us in the meantime.

I got to play pharmacy aide and nurse last week. They were short-staffed, and I had a week off of language. So it worked out fine except that I haven't done any nursing in ages! (And the drugs in the pharmacy were mainly in French!) I also worked on getting the divider curtains finished for the wards. I got two sets done and have two more to go.

Have been getting your letters again. Just found out you had the flu the first of last month!

Love,

Shirley

P.S. Pastor Paul and Apolline got married! She is a lovely Christian woman, and we are so happy for them.

March 19, 1986 Newsletter

Greetings from Togo!

Luke got up at 4 a.m. Monday morning and went to Kpalimé to see Haley's comet. I was awake when Bob came home this morning about 4:30 a.m. We went out and did some star gazing! It was a beautiful night. The sky was full of stars, but the mountain made it impossible to see the comet.

Meanwhile, our seven-year-old John has been very burdened for the people he sees when he goes back into the bush to play.

"Mommy, please, we need to start a Bible study in the jungle where I go to play!" he said.

Later the same day, he went to his teacher, "Miss Thayer, I don't know enough Bible words in French. How come we can't learn some more at school? I need to start a Bible study back in the bush where I play!"

Kelli patiently explained to John that Isabelle, the French lady who comes to teach three times a week, isn't a Christian herself. She wouldn't think to teach Bible terms. Later the same week, the subject was brought up again with Bob. John continued asking each chance he got until at last Bob had a break in his work, and off they went on their bikes—John, Bob, and the three brothers. John's main concern was for some people at a small cluster of huts off the main road.

After a rather roundabout ride, they found themselves greeted and welcomed into a compound. Two men prayed to receive Christ that afternoon and have continued to show interest in weekly Bible study and church attendance. I don't think they were quite who John was thinking of, but God knows and directs. We praise the Lord for the burden He has given John for the lost around us!

School business has kept me out of trouble. It takes so much time for me to stay on top of what happens with our money. We will, eventually, have a nice school building for our children!

The tractor is down again, and so is the hospital lawnmower. The rains are coming, and we are looking pretty shaggy again. We could use a full-time mechanic person just to keep out here! Dave Moody, the printer on our team, comes up on Tuesday and Thursday and does a great job. He does maintenance on the generators for Bob, and that's a tremendous help. But send someone over who would love to do this kind of work everyday!

Bradley Washer is here and talking a mile a minute while I type. It has been a while since I've had to do two things simultaneously, and I'm having a little trouble concentrating on this note.

Oh, I just have five minutes to get to the hospital, get some copies of this, and get them in envelopes to send off.

Take care. We love you all.

Love,

Shirley

P.S. In my Bible study this afternoon, we started on the first chapter of Colossians. We talked about God and His preeminence. Mrs. Dzgali said, "You know people here have a real problem believing in God when they can't see or hear Him."

"Oh," I said, "but they can't hear their gods. They can only see them because they are made out of wood."

Her comment was that you can see *and* hear the fetish gods through the wooden idols. They make noises, not understandable words, but sounds! It was just another reminder that the evil spirits are very active here. The more I go to the village, the more aware I am of all the satanic forces that are alive and active in people's lives. I know we have God's protection, but continue to pray.

We also talked about how hard it is to have patience and long-suffering with joyfulness! Honestly, I am having a hard time with this, too.

May 8, 1986

Hi Mom,

Today when we were headed for Kpodzi, Guardian came and said our little Papa Ayte died. Do you remember me telling you about an old man who comes to Kpodzi church? He professed Christ as Savior. When he was baptized, he came up clapping and said, "Once I served Satan, but now I know God and serve Him!"

He has been so faithful to come to all of the services even though he hasn't been well. He was admitted to the hospital last week. Bob had done all he could medically, so we were going to take him back to his home.

A big hesitation for people joining our church is where they will be buried if they leave the Catholic church. Non-Catholics get buried in the pagan and fetish grounds. No one wants that, so Bob left Papa Ayte's body here. He will ask the Chief to give us a Christian cemetery. I don't know if it can happen fast enough to be useful for today. Bob and I just talked about this concern. We said it should be high up on the list of things to get accomplished before leaving for our furlough home this summer.

I stayed home this morning. I have been having a lot of pain behind my eyes, and my stomach is upset. Maybe malaria? I decided to rest. I have a hard time sleeping with so many people around the house and grounds during the week.

Bob helped the boys get a ladder made for the treehouse yesterday. It is so high up, and now I pray that they get the sides up on the thing before one of the kids falls out! Now that the brush is all cleared, I can see it very well. It didn't look so high when I couldn't see the ground under it. Ha!

Must close and get dinner going.

Love,

Shirley

July 6, 1986

Hi again,

The days have been full of the routine and everything else too. On Sunday, I went with Andrea and Jean (both part of a nursing team that came to Togo as part of their school curriculum in the States) and the boys to Kpodzi. On our way, Bob flagged me down and asked if I could go to Agou for an anti-D serum that they needed before noon. *No problem.* We kept going and picked up a hospital employee named Felix. He told us that Pastor Paul was sick. Andrea had planned on giving her testimony to the kids' class that morning, but she needed a translator. After arriving, we were told Pastor Paul was coming anyway and that he would translate. So I left them and kept going. (Pastor Paul didn't come, and instead, the Ghana lady, who is with the Assembly of God and learning Ewe, translated while nursing her baby.) Felix translated for the sermon. He sure doesn't know much English, so I am unsure what word went forth this morning. OH ME!

Meanwhile, the lady we did an emergency bowel resection on was in trouble. When I got back to give the medicine to Bob, he was driving out on the tractor to find a nurse so that he could take the lady back to surgery. (The tractor was the only working vehicle at the time.) I gave him the medicine and started on my search for a nurse. As I came back to the hospital, the lady arrested. Unfortunately, she didn't make it to the OR.

The boys took their bikes apart to paint them so they can sell them before we leave for furlough. I hope it is worth all of the time they have invested in it. Right now, they are out having a squirt gun fight with large syringes. It rained hard and long yesterday, and they were mud from head to foot!

I can't believe we'll be back in the States soon! Must close to get dinner on for the kids and ready for church.

Love,

Shirley

October 1986 Newsletter

BUT can it be? As the wheels and turbine engines of KLM Flight 657 came to a stop, it hardly seemed possible that we were home. Our families hugged us and treated us to our favorite hamburger. It slowly became clear that we were back in the good old U.S.A. There were no goats, chickens, ducks, nor people to dodge as we drove. The shelves in every store were piled high with endless varieties of goods of all descriptions. No doubt about it. There's only one place on planet earth like it!

THANKS to everyone who helped us find and settle into our home during furlough, just one-half mile from our home church. People generously provided food, furniture, furnishings, and financial assistance.

BE or not to be a doctor again? With unprecedented speed, another answer to prayer, the state of Michigan reinstated Bob's medical license so that he could begin advanced training in orthopedic and urologic surgery, along with emergency medicine in Ann Arbor while home on furlough. What a privilege to be so warmly offered, by many of Bob's former surgical colleagues, the specialized training he was seeking.

TO be back in a Christian school in America has been a very positive experience for our boys. Because of the excellent education they received in Togo, their adjustments to school have been outstanding, and all are doing fine. Both Luke and Matthew have been on the soccer team and are now enjoying basketball.

GOD continues to encourage us greatly. What a blessing to see faithful prayer partners who daily prayed for us. It is also a thrill to witness young people who are willing to present their lives for His service!

But thanks be to God! We praise the Lord for our Togolese nationals who write and tell us of their own growth and of those being reached for the gospel at the hospital. Pastor Paul recently wrote of the death of his mother, his wife's miscarriage, and other items of discouragement in the work at Kpodzi. Please pray that the power of God may be upon his life and ministry.

Love,

Shirley

March 1987 Newsletter

Dear Praying Friends,

It hardly seems possible that eight months have passed, and we are making departure plans for the early part of August. Our basement and garage are overflowing with supplies and equipment!

We are grateful for a farmer in our church who allowed us to use one of his buildings for storage. Last week we began filling it up as we picked up our first load of hospital supplies. In addition to that, a hospital in Petoskey, Michigan, donated a lovely ultrasound machine!

We have been encouraged by recent letters and events in Togo. During February, Togo celebrated its 20-year anniversary under President Eyadéma who has maintained stability and provided essential freedoms for his country.

We are most grateful for the liberty to freely proclaim the gospel!

Love,

Shirley

August 9, 1987

Dear Mom,

Our return to Togo has been super. Things are, of course, more worn-in at the house. But it was clean, and the previous occupants had made the beds. So we are just resettling as we can instead of cleaning just to function. The container doesn't come until August 20, so I have a little time to settle before that chaos ensues.

The yard here was beautiful when we arrived. It is in the rainy season, so everything is green and lush. All the starter plants have matured. Our pine tree, which was only a foot when we left, is now five feet tall! The rose trellis is covered, as are the walls of the garage with sweet pea vines. The ferns have all done great, too. The grass is thick.

Carrie, who has joined us for the school year, continues to be a blessing. She is going through a lot of adjustments, but I'm confident she will be fine. What 15-year-old girl wouldn't have a few hurdles coming to a new country?

Some of our church people from Kpozdi were at the airport and then a lot were at the church when we came the next day. They gave us such an enthusiastic welcome back. Some were missing, and we understand they have stopped coming. That was sad for us to learn.

Bob told everyone all year that it wasn't any hotter in Togo than at home in Michigan. He decided he was wrong! Guess it wouldn't be nice to say, "I told you so!"

Church is at 6:30, so I guess I'd better call the kids in to get ready.

Love,

Shirley

August 18, 1987

Dear Mom,

Saturday was a very traumatic day for me. Bob came and asked if I'd help Dr. Dave in the OR with an emergency C-section. The other nurses had left for the market, and he needed to help another family. It was with much reluctance that I consented to help.

I had just got changed and heard someone yell, "Code!" A little girl had come in with cerebral malaria, and she arrested. Dr. Dave was there and started CPR. I got the bag. We worked an hour but could't get her back. Meanwhile, the lady who needed the C-section was in distress. The fetal heart tones were dropping with every contraction. To make a long story short, I ended up doing medications and vitals because the other nurses had to work on the baby. The baby never did breathe on its own. They brought the baby out with an ambu bag, but the baby never made it. Adelale, the mother, is grieving but okay physically.

Following that, a little girl came in with a snake bite. She was unconscious and hemorrhaging everywhere. Susan, who set up the laboratory at the hospital, did a type on her, and they just went ahead and gave her blood with a crossmatch. Praise the Lord! In less than an hour, she was awake and alert. We found out that her family goes to KpaKope to church, another ABWE church plant. The fetishers came and wanted to do their rituals, but the father stood firm. He told them that he would pray to God and get his child to the hospital. Pray for him because he may be under a lot of pressure now!

I'm waiting now for Mercy to come so that we can go to the hospital and visit Adelale, the lady whose baby died. She is grieving much more than most Togolese appear to grieve. Mercy and I visited her yesterday. Adelale is Catholic and knows a lot of the correct answers.

We explained the gospel and left her with a tract. She asked us to return today. It is 4 p.m., so I guess I'd better look for Mercy. I'll need to feed this crew pretty soon.

Love,

Shirley

P.S. I'm adding this to give you the "rest of the story." Mercy was tired, so I went on my own. Adelale was so much better and happy to see me, even if our conversation was short. I gave balloons to the kids and, in general, just kept smiling!

September 29, 1987

Dear Mom,

It is Tuesday afternoon, and we are at the school. This job of facilitating students isn't really too exciting, but it has been a joy at the same time. I never would have believed that I could do it; and, indeed, I couldn't without the help of our Lord! The kids are doing okay. I do have some minor concerns about paying attention to details and studying all of the materials before they take a test, but I think they will see the need after they get back their first tests. I can only check to see that they did all of the questions and when I do, it seems they are getting the general idea about things, but I do see with my "untrained" eye little mistakes.

The high schoolers have decided that they would like to have a ministry in some way. We are going to talk with the people at the kitchen area (patient families) once a week after school. Perhaps we'll have a cuisine ministry of sharing with those who want to listen. It will be a lot of work for me, but I feel the need to begin a ministry with the Togolese as well. Bob is working on a class to give to our leaders on how to witness to different groups of people. It focuses on culturally offensive things because of beliefs, etc. I am going to have the high schoolers take it, too.

Have I written to you since Matthew fell from the rope swing? Actually, the rope broke, and he broke a couple of ribs. It happened last Thursday, and we have spent some uncomfortable moments. He had a lot of trouble breathing at first. He also had a temp on Friday, so I had Mr. Dzagli do a malaria smear. Matthew was put on a strong dose of medication, but yesterday the headaches were back. It scares me because malaria has taken so many lives since our return and seems to be uncontrolled, even with medication.

John woke up with pink eye this morning. Adzovi has been off work all week, so I am getting worn out without house help. Tomorrow I am supposed to teach for Diane, so that means I will have the four older elementary age kids as well as my high schoolers! Somehow, I will figure out how to get a break.

Carrie and I are going to Lomé on Friday to do errands and also get groceries. Carrie wants to call home. She called once right after we got here, and we will not be able to afford it too many times. I think that is hard for her to understand since her dad is a doctor *with money*!

Take care and give our greetings to all.

Love,

Shirley

P.S. It's now Oct. 4. Oh, Mom. I've been so discouraged. I'd just like to come home to the States and be loved! John is back in school, but Joshua has pink eye now.

October 27, 1987

Dear Mom,

It is Tuesday already and I can see that I may not get much French in again this week. I think Bob has treated me for about everything; so, hopefully, I will come to the end of what we call the "ailments"! Ha. He started giving me shots on Sunday because the sore on my leg was bad with a red streak going down the front of my leg. The spot is starting to dry up and the red has receded, so maybe just a couple more shots will do it.

Yesterday we had some excitement here at the school. I was giving Luke his typing drills and all of a sudden something dropped behind me. It was a green mamba! Luke calmly said, "Sit still, Mom." When it had slithered away from us, he went for the broom. By the time he got back with the broom, the snake had crawled into a corner and started up the side of the cupboard and into a crack between the wall and cupboard! Needless to say, school was disrupted. Luke and Mensaga tried to entice it out but nothing worked. Steve Anderson ended up working with a mirror and flashlight to locate it. Taking the cabinet loose, they used a BB gun, *coupe coupe*, and other assorted instruments. They finally got it out about 2 p.m. Typing class is at 10:30 a.m., so that was a three and a half hour recess! But no one was hurt. Thank you, Lord!

On the other pest front, our very aggressive mouse is getting braver all the time. Bob stays up at night trying to catch the thing. He usually sees it, but it is too fast. It eats the bait off the traps without getting caught when they spring.

It chewed the tops off of my wooden spoons and spatulas and ate a hole through the top of one of my cereal containers! It's getting braver. Last night, while the kids were studying, before the generator went off, it was out and about! None of the the kids could catch it! I don't like it one bit. Last night Bob went and got some surgical scrub paper that is very sticky and put a cookie in the middle. Hopefully, that will get him.

It is almost 3 p.m. We have the high school cuisine ministry this afternoon, so I'll write later.

Love,

Shirley

November 19, 1987 Newsletter

Dear Mom,

Ants, cockroaches, rats, snakes, and scorpions—resistant malaria, pneumonia, cuts requiring stitches, broken ribs, and persistent infections—HOT, HOT, HOT days filled with dust! The once beautiful countryside around me has succumbed to the hot, dry days and become brown and lifeless. I admit to feeling dried up and discouraged in the past several months! Please forgive me and continue to pray for God's sustaining grace, peace, and comfort in our lives. He has blessed our ministries and continues to work in lives, both ours and those around us!

That snake—the green mamba—that dropped in at school a couple of weeks ago has a papa! The generators were acting up and I came out of school to go pull the main switch at the house (to save the appliances) and just about stepped on him. He was coming out of the school yard and heading across the road. A good rule of thumb is to always watch where you are walking, and I didn't follow it. Instead, I was gazing at the black smoke pouring out of the generator shack! I called Luke, but that snake was so big it even stifled Luke's eagerness to be the hero! It started off fast, so we let it go. But that means he is still out there! Needless to say, I am watching where I step these days.

The cuisine ministry that the high school students have been involved with continues each week. We have been studying in the book of Ephesians in Bible class and talking about how to keep our Christian walk alive. Yesterday we had the privilege of seeing two men accept Christ as their Savior. The students came to school today very excited! May God keep their hearts and lives aflame as they see Him draw others to Himself through their lives.

At the cuisine, a mother tossed me her fussy, little guy who was distracting other listeners. Being unsure of myself but willing, I took the little guy so that others could listen. He settled down, and we began visiting people who were nearby but not listening to the Bible story. I'll be, if that little kid didn't close the gap! With no diaper, he relieved himself in my arms. Urine dripped off my elbow. All those reluctant ladies came to my aid and even began to listen to the Bible story! I have allowed Satan to discourage me with all of the things I can't do (especially in the area of communication). I have felt the burden to just do what I can and let God do the rest! His ways are not our ways, but what a story today was!

Carrie is giving a piano lesson. Luke is at the workshop. I'm out of news so guess I'll close.

Love,

Shirley

January 5, 1988

Dear Mom,

It is hard to believe that Christmas is over, and we started another year! The children are all back at the books and into a routine. They all seem to have enjoyed the vacation and are ready to study once again, as prepared as boys can be at ages 14, 12, 11, and 8. (Plus, Carrie, who is living with us for the school year. She's 15.)

One evening during vacation, we had five Cropseys in the OR helping. Josh was my first assistant (we were both scrubbed in). I looked over, and he looked green. I asked him if he was okay, and he said, "I think my stomach is tickling me."

He sat a while with this head between his knees. That helped a lot.

The harmattan has been very heavy. The dust and smoke are thick in the air. Many people struggle with respiratory problems. Bob has had trouble with his asthma for the first time in years. Often our night's sleep is interrupted by Guardian who pleads for the doctor to come quickly. Measles, malaria, typhoid, and pneumonia take lives daily. Croup is getting many children, too. It rains soot upon us daily from the many fires that burn uncontrolled around us. The days are sweltering. Everything is brown now. The nights, on the contrary, are pretty cool.

Carrie is going to be with us for another five months. She has gone through many adjustments but is becoming more and more a part of our family. She gives piano lessons and participates in the cuisine ministry. It has been a growing experience for us all to add a 15-year-old girl to the household. She turned 16 at the beginning of January, and we had a time of fellowship with cake and ice cream. Mark T. made her a driver's license, and Uncle Steve came with a banner that said, "Happy SWEET 16, Carrie!"

Love,

Shirley

January 26, 1988 Newsletter

Dear Mom,

The dust lay heavy in the air as we made our way down the footpath from the church to the tiny village of Kpodzi. Children from the school shouted out, "*Yovo. Yovo. Bonjour! Est-ce que ça se passe bien? Merci!*" Susan and I followed

Adzovi and Pastor Paul's wife, Apolline, to the compound of three different families, each with a story to tell from life's journey.

Mama A. greeted us with her usual big smile and friendly manner. A child cried in the corner and snuggled up to her mom, frightened from the sight of a strange white person. Sitting across the compound, another lady came into view. She is an unbeliever who suffered great pain from hemorrhoids and could no longer walk. My eyes met her empty stare. This lady has been mixed up with fetish. With some reluctance, the ladies went over to tell the lady with hemorrhoids that perhaps she could get relief if she would come to the hospital. We also left a tract with an explanation of the gospel.

We listened to Mama A. I asked her to give us her testimony. She shared it with much emotion for a person close to her had just died without Jesus. Then she said she worries because she can't remember the things she learned in church when at her house. We shared some Scripture from 1 Peter and prayed together.

On our way to the next compound, an older man who regularly attends the church intercepted us. He begged us to come to his compound and greet his family. His daughter, just four days earlier, had a baby die from measles. She attended church when we first started having services but had gone back to the Catholic church. She said she is now ashamed and afraid to return. It was good to tell her that the Word of God is our guide and comfort. The man says that he is the only believer in his family and asked, "Who will tell my family when I die, too?" Apolline used the opportunity to go through the plan of salvation with this group of people. Pray for Mr. K's household.

Out the opening in the mud wall, down the path, and around the big village meeting tree, we went. The odor of palm wine was strong. Its influence was very evident, even at 10 a.m. Winding down and around several more compounds, we came to a sorry sight. A lady that was once very large sat with head down and eyes closed, smelling wretched. She had attended church and gotten medicine to help her eyes. They had gotten better, but she ran out of the medication and didn't come back. She is blind now and without family to care for her. She has one son who lives in Ghana, but when she has someone write, he says he will not come. When she became a Christian, she gave up all of her fetish activities and destroyed all her fetishes. I wish I could say the church has made it better for her, but we are still working on improving the situation. I am going to try to get someone from the Blind Center to give her mobility training. Pastor Paul will have someone from the church fetch her water and help her get washed daily.

Coming home, we had some excellent conversation centered around our Almighty God. We discussed how God is in control and that He can meet all needs and give comfort and peace in all situations! I am so inadequate for any of these situations, but I know that God cares more than I know how to manage or help.

In other news, Bob was in an accident last Saturday. He was between two curves at a point in the road where it dropped off a yard on the edge. A taxi full of people came barreling around the curve and into the suburban side and the trailer full of wood. There were no bad injuries, and we just got some scratches on the truck and a flat tire on the trailer. It, of course, took the better part of his day and will still take more time with the police.

Must close.

Love,

Shirley

February 17, 1988 Newsletter

Dear Mom,

I thank the Lord for giving me renewed health. I feel very rested and able to keep up with the schedule of school, language, Bible studies, and village visitation.

The cuisine ministry with the high school students is going well. They use many visuals from last semester and repeat some of the stories, so it is not as time-consuming with the preparations now. We continue to have good attendance, and Mr. Dzagli has remained faithful to translate for us.

The boys are all doing just fine. John used all of his allowances from the past months, and now he has a rabbit. MK friend Ben also decided to do the same, so now they have a daddy and a mommy. Guess what they think will happen? They are going into the bunny selling business!

Love,

Shirley

March 24, 1988 Newsletter

Dear Mom,

Greetings from Togo!

The odor was less than fresh—the heat sweltering. And my Togolese sisters in Christ were teaching me about true service with joyfulness. Adzovi and Mercy sang praises to God. Neither of them attend our church at Kpodzi, but both were willing to help our old, Blind Mama. (Our ladies at Kpodzi became unwilling to keep up their meal schedule because Mama was incontinent and her room was in terrible condition. So Susan and I and another Kpodzi woman said we would clean them and get her some attention.)

The conditions did not offer any earthly reward. Some fetishers even threatened us. "If you go into those rooms, great evil will fall upon you," they warned us.

"Our God is able to protect us," Susan said, and then we scrubbed that room from top to bottom. (I have been praying for God's protection, even in my moments of doubting.) Sunday we heard that the young niece of Blind Mama beat her and hit her in the back of the head with a block. She decided since the rooms were clean, she would like to get her out and live there herself. Because Mama is old and blind, we have been counseled to seek help from the Chief in this situation. Pray for God's wisdom in trying to help her in the best way!

Monday I joined the wives of pastors in the Kpalimé area. We shared prayer requests, concerns, and then spent time in the Word. It is always a time of encouragement for me. Please pray for Pastor John's wife. She can't read, and it makes it difficult for her to shepherd the woman in her congregation. My heart's desire is to see one of the other pastor's wives that can read take her under her wing.

I need patience in this area and His direction in how and when to encourage the ladies down these lines.

Love,

Shirley

April 10, 1988

Dear Mom,

This weekend the rain "beat" down on us. I learned in my Ewe class that you don't get wet in the rain. It "beats you." After watching a couple of the previous storms take shape, it is easier to see why they say it "beats you"! I so appreciate being able to keep up with language study in the midst of the activity. I am not too sure that I will ever be fluent, but it would be nice not to be in the dark all the time! My Togolese friends encourage me and keep me learning. They are patient, loving, and kind.

Our little old Blind Mama is doing all she can to make it impossible for us to help her. I would love to report good news, but without a miracle, we can't do any more to help her.

This last Saturday, Ann Washer and I did a surprise luncheon for Susan, who is leaving the field of Togo. Yes, it is the Susan I talk about all the time in my adventures at Kpodzi. Susan, my very proper friend from the southern U.S. who makes me laugh until I cry and always has a cheerful word to say. Bob and I are going to miss her. My heart is broken, and it is most difficult to see her packing and getting ready to leave next Sunday evening. Mark Thompson is also leaving next week. He has been out for his third short-term stint, and the boys will have a big void when he goes. (He is living with us now until he leaves.) Mark prepared dinner for us yesterday. It was not just boiling water; it was turkey, potatoes, gravy, two veggies, rolls, and a cherry-topped cheesecake. It was beautiful and such a special encouragement to me. What an example to my boys too!

Perhaps one of the most challenging things about foreign missions is giving yourself to others and then watching them leave. Saying goodbye is tough.

On Sunday I arrived at church to find that Pastor Paul and Apolline had been called to Lomé for an emergency. Pastor Paul had a believer preach who has had a difficult time with some of the biblical concepts. Culturally, as a woman and not understanding a lot of what he was saying, I didn't feel I could do anything. He closed the service with an altar call but had the elders pray for the salvation of all who came forward! He asked why Susan and I weren't going to come forward, and she said that we didn't understand. He made one effort to explain, and then we knew we had a problem. We just told him he needed to close the service in prayer, and it was not the appropriate time for us to discuss the situation. After church, I briefly explained that salvation is an individual decision and that no one can do that for someone else. Bob will go this afternoon to talk to him. What a challenge to teach and train God's ways to a people who often just want to add it onto whatever else they believe.

This letter is turning into the chapter of a book. Thank you for your prayers and for the many ways you show us God's love.

Love,

Shirley

May 17, 1988

Dear Mom,

The boys are back in school today after missing two days. Friday we took them all to Lomé to see Carrie Hyink (the girl who lived with us this last school year) and her mother and grandmother (who came to pick her up) off to the States.

While she was here, Carrie's mom, Linda, also had the chance to follow me in my weekly routine: visitation at Kpodzi and the hospital, church at Kpodzi, language study, and Bible studies. A highlight was seeing Carrie share at the cuisine ministry. I thank the Lord for the special time that He allowed us to share!

It is lunchtime! Must go.

Love,

Shirley

May 30, 1988

Dear Mom,

There are another ten people leaving tonight for the States, so I am getting mail ready to send with them. I have just about gotten caught up from the two weeks I didn't write any letters when Carrie's mom, Linda, was here.

Things are settling down and back to "normal." It is just that back to normal hasn't changed a thing! Bob and Dr. Dave struggle over what is too much for the nursing staff. Bob sent a patient to Agou Saturday night (Bob was the one on call) because they had done 19 cases in the last 48 hours, and he thought the staff was loaded up.

It is payday, and because of the cutbacks (then the added overtime for emergencies), there isn't enough money! Same old story, "Too much work, too little staff, no funds!" Keep praying because this place isn't going to float unless we are all behind the necessary changes and willing to develop alternatives. Yesterday the medical committee set up a point system for the nurses so that the the doctors will know when the workload has hit maximum. I trust that will help with the friction. They also came up with a program to present to churches back home to raise money, but that will not come in for another six months.

I will stop taking language class for a while until my head clears up or the schedule lets up some. I am having a tough time keeping up these days. Also, with the kids off for summer break, I need to be here and do some special things with them.

They are growing up so quickly!

Love,

Shirley

June 15, 1988

Dear Mom,

This has been a full day. In fact, I overplanned and didn't make it to prayer meeting. I've never done that before.

I got home late from Kpalimé and needed to bake a birthday cake for Joshua. I was making a taco salad for supper, so I soaked and cleaned food from the market, fried hamburger, soured cream, and grated cheese. Then I popped the cake in the oven. I knew I was cutting it short. Later I noticed I never turned on the oven! I hadn't put in the water either. He wanted a bundt cake, so I decided I'd better get it done right. It came out just about the time church was over.

We got Joshua a set of homing pigeons for his birthday. A missionary up north raised them. They are purebred and beautiful birds. Bob got a large cage made for them yesterday, so we are all set. Martha and the kids are going to go swimming with us tomorrow to help celebrate.

The hospital is in a bind financially. The home office is asking someone to come home to raise funds. They are going to help us for three months and no more.

Meanwhile, we are all "pulling in." The generator is going to be off from 1 p.m. to 5 p.m. to save fuel costs. We missionaries will "adopt-an-employee" for salaries and other creative ideas we can think of.

I think and pray for you often. My joints ache along with my head during the rainy season. It reminds me of you! Take care!

Love,

Shirley

June 22, 1988 Newsletter

Greetings from the land of Togo,

The sun is shining, and God has given us a light, refreshing breeze! The rainy season is here. I was helping John learn his memory verse for Bible school. Revelation 4:11 says, "Worthy are You, our Lord and our God, to receive glory and honor and power; for You created all things, and because of Your will they existed, and were created."

Many of you have prayed for our Blind Mama in Kpodzi. She went home to be with the Lord last week.

It seems that the evil one will distract us from doing God's work in any way that He can. We have cut back on the patient load to give more time for spiritual ministries. Now the staff has been busy revamping a budget to fit the smaller income. The stress level is high among the missionary staff, and we appreciate your prayers that our lives would glorify our Lord. Someone will go Stateside to do some fundraising soon, per the request of the home office.

The two beautiful homing pigeons Joshua got for his birthday— Something ate them! Probably army ants. It was gross. Ron gave the boys another python. It was so active and too big for my comfort, so Matt let it go last night.

Have enjoyed our visit this afternoon!

Love,

Shirley

July 12, 1988

Dear Mom,

A faithful member of our Kpodzi church, Celestine, shared that his father died yesterday morning. Just one week earlier we went to visit him because his second wife died, cause unknown. Celestine's dad responded in a positive way. He said that if he should die, he knew that he would go to heaven. He had asked the Lord to forgive him of his sin and come into his life. That was the first day he had indicated that he had made a decision for Christ. His tumor had advanced to the point that it was difficult for him to talk. Celestine's mother, the two small orphan children from Celestine's dad's second wife, and several other girls from the compound attended church the next Sunday and several times since.

We went to the wake for Celestine's father that night. We left the wake early but still didn't get home until almost midnight. We were given front-row seats, and I found it very interesting. He was buried this morning. Bob always thinks of something and said, "Just think how much the tourist would have to pay to see this sort of thing from a front-row seat!" We were all very tired after all the activity but thankful we were able to support Celestine.

Love,

Shirley

August 2, 1988

Dear Mom,

The weather remains cool and rainy here in Togo. It sounds like our temperatures have been lower than yours!

The week of July 18 we held Bible school at Kpodzi. By Tuesday there were over 200 kids! On Wednesday, we had 158 kids inside and 52 kids watching from the window. I asked Pastor Paul what was happening. Why were some of the kids not coming inside? He said the children watching from the outside would just listen. They were beat by their church leaders for attending the day before. Many of those children came all week to listen to the gospel, and we saw 69 children make decisions for Christ. My heart broke more than once. A 12-year-old girl stood up and shared that she had accepted Christ, despite being beaten, and she knew God would help her. Some of our leaders said that we should not allow the children to listen if they don't have permission from their parents. I don't feel it was wrong to let them listen, but we certainly must teach those who believe biblical principles. Oh how we need God's wisdom in helping them grow in their new lives in Christ!

There were about 87 kids in Sunday school and church this morning. I gave all 12 of my Togolese leaders follow-up material to use with those who made decisions. What a joy to see the leaders and their groups after church this morning—discipling!

The summer has brought lots of people our way. A quick glance at the calendar says we served 57 extra meals at our table last month and had nine overnight guests. Matt and Josh took a taxi last Monday up to Kara to spend two weeks with Denny Washer. That experience will give them a lot to share! Joshua now has nine assorted birds. He had 11 before he left but two babies died! What a birdman.

Luke has fixed three lawnmowers that were retired and at present, he has the suburban all taken apart and is doing "body repair" work to repaint it. The boys along with the Anderson children painted the school inside this summer, and the boys and I did a lot of work at the warehouse for the hospital.

In their spare time, they wear out the sports court. You could say we have stayed busy this summer!

Love,

Shirley

October 10, 1988

Dear Mom,

My writing is a bit worse than usual, so bear with me. The Lord is blessing in wonderful ways, and the evil one is not so happy.

You know that our workload has been considerable since July. Joshua was ill for most of August and hospitalized toward the end of the month. Thank the Lord he is feeling better, but he's still thin.

My head has been bad for about six weeks. A couple of weeks ago, the docs gave me steroids to relieve the symptoms. The medication gave me a wonderful boost of energy. That Monday I took a paralyzed lady to Lomé. It has been downhill since then.

I took a blood test. I feel very much like I did in Québec that first year of language school. We don't have the right reagents to do a test for mono, but Bob feels that is what I have from looking at the blood smear. I've stayed in bed all week and as usual, everyone has been super to help us out.

Bob was summoned to court. Do you remember when Bob got hit by a taxi near Kpalimé last Christmas? Bob found out the driver is suing because of a cut on his nose! That was Wednesday. Friday Bob went to talk to the lawyer. I trust that all of these small trials will conform us to His Image. It is a comfort to know that God in control of all things.

Adzovi has kept the household going. She does laundry, ironing, cleaning, and some cooking. I thank the Lord for her! Kwadzo, her three-year-old son, comes with her now and keeps me entertained in the morning when I'm awake.

Mr. Dzalgi stopped yesterday after the ward service and reported that 20 people prayed to receive Christ. He was especially excited about two who asked what they should do with their idols. He said, "Praise the Lord! That is the Holy Spirit at work!" There were 21 decisions the previous week, too.

Must close and lie down. I'll try to keep you posted.

Love,

Shirley

P.S. Matt got a baby monkey, but the monkey is sick. So we are watching him for rabies. He is in a cage now. Poor Matt doesn't have very good luck with pets.

December 10, 1988 Newsletter

Dear Mom,

What a whirlwind of activities! In light of all that has happened in the last three months, this letter must be a letter of thanksgiving. I am so quick to give God thanks when things are going as I think they should, but I will praise Him no matter the season!

While I lay flat in my bed in Togo, so many people took care of my family and me. There was a 24-hour prayer chain, a friend who came just to sit with me, a couple who came and said, "How can we help?" There was a group of Togolese ladies who sang praises in Ewe through my bedroom window. Another friend stopped by to visit and read God's Word.

There were, "You provide the meal, and I'll cook. Together we'll dine!" and "I'll bake some Christmas cookies for you," along with "I'll make your son's costume for the Christmas play."

The list goes on and on. I am so grateful for the help and love of those around us in Togo.

Then, God arranged our quick, medical trip home to the States and back to be uneventful with luggage arriving in both directions! There were helpful people all along the way and splendid health care in between! A neurologist went after my problem with both barrels, and I had tests done which often take weeks before they can be scheduled.

Seven years ago, I was ill with encephalitis, secondary to mono. The test I had while in the States showed that I had a viral infection and much cortical irritation. To state it plainly, I am still fighting the same old problem. It has gotten progressively better, but I still struggle with symptoms. A verse I have claimed over the years is Psalm 119:75, "I know, Lord, that Your judgments are righteous, And that You have afflicted me in faithfulness."

My thoughts are often mixed, but I can always find God waiting in my spiral to give comfort and peace as I allow Him. It was not easy for me to come back to the mission field, but we know this is where God would have us for now.

Psalm 94:19 says, "When my anxious thoughts multiply within me, Your comfort delights my soul."

I can't give this letter a storybook ending in the world's eyes. Today finds Bob back to his regular schedule and the boys spending extra time talking with me flopped across the foot of my bed, which seems to be my permanent residence for now. My head symptoms have not changed. The medication has not settled well, and so the struggle continues. Whether I am in the valley or soaring above the mountain tops, God is there with me.

I thank God that I am able to be His child. Now that's a true storybook ending!

Love,

Shirley

P.S. Mom, I am so glad you came to the airport even if I slept most of the drive. I never will like goodbyes; they break my heart every time.

April 3, 1989

Dear Mom,

It was so good to hear your voice! Thank you so much for calling me back just because I needed to hear you. Mail has been napping on its way to us!

You know how difficult it was for us to return to Togo last November. There were the financial burdens along with my health concerns. But, the Lord has worked in His way to meet all of the other expenses we know of right now!

One of our churches sent in $1,000 and another church $2,000. That covered our $1,640 deficit and paid some medical bills not covered by insurance.

What a privilege to step out in faith, believing God to supply.

Love,

Shirley

April 12, 1989

Dear Mom,

I just returned home from the village of Kpodzi. It is the first time I've visited since last September. What a joy! Pastor Paul's wife, Apolline, takes Mrs. Kwassi each week and teaches her just like we started out. It is such a thrill to see her pass on and teach the ladies what she is learning. So few of them speak French, so I'm very limited to do it myself. Talk about tongues! The four of us made a sight. Mrs. Kwassi speaks another tribal language Kabiyé; Adzovi speaks Mina; Apolline Ewe; and I, English. It sure makes one realize it is the Lord who gives the increase in spite of us! Good news, though! One lady we visited, Afi, prayed to receive Christ this morning.

We visited another lady who had a teething baby who didn't want to nurse so she was engorged and miserable. Isn't all the world the same?

Love,

Shirley

April 25, 1989

Dear Mom,

I might describe the day as one long, sauna bath. It was HOT and muggy, with temperatures up in the high 90s by 8 a.m. It may resemble a hothouse, but the countryside is beautiful!

Kpodzi visitation continues to be a highlight of my week. Tomorrow morning, we will go for our second follow-up study with Afi. Oh, Mom! My ability in French is so limited, and it was so difficult. Last week was a heartbreaker for all of us. Afi is partially crippled, and when she went to sit on the low stool, she lost her balance and fell. She has many thoughts to work through with her new God. In the past, she offered sacrifices and paid fetish priests to have the gods help, but they didn't.

"Can't my new God heal me?" she asks us.

All her motives, thoughts, and feelings—only God knows the heart. We wept together many times as we looked into God's Word and shared the treasures that can be hers. The Togolese do not often show sorrow, so it was touching to see the ladies affected by Afi's life. Pray for us as we continue to help Afi grow to know her Lord better.

Bob says we are going to hire another part-time house helper to get through the summer. That sounds great, but it will take patience to train before that person is helpful. And we don't have a lot of time. Pray that I would be able to do this pleasing unto the Lord and that our summer would be a ministry to many (and in order)!

Bob put up another Tarzan swing at the school last week. The kids practice basketball these days. I guess baseball season is over here!

They go in their own cycles with activities.

Love,

Shirley

May 6, 1989

Dear Mom,

I've had one new cultural experience after another the past couple of weeks: casket making, a village trial on behalf of a dead girl, a funeral, and last Wednesday morning, I went for Bob to his trial case from the taxi accident that happened over a year ago.

Let me start with the casket making. Mensaga's sister died, and he came here about 6 a.m. He needed someone to take him north to pick up the casket. It was to a village where his father used to teach and where he had several family members. Bob sent me with the hospital truck.

In the process, I learned how to make a casket and followed Mensaga and his other sister everywhere. I enjoyed a 2-liter bottle of Fanta pop and discovered that you swallow fufu and you chew rice. We also had a yummy goat sauce, foot and all. This was all before 8 a.m.

On the way back to Atime, where the body was, we picked up clothes and many passengers. After the usual greetings and sitting with the body, I rushed off to Kpodzi.

In Kpodzi, Adzovi helped me make food purchases at the market to support the family. We returned at 3 p.m. for the funeral but instead found a village trial! The discussion was heated. Don't ask me what it was all about. But after it was over, I will never forget the sound of the family hammering the top of the casket and shoveling the dirt on top. It is so final here—what a vivid reminder of our need for the Savior.

Bob's long-awaited court case came up again this week. This is the third time we've gone to court for the accident Bob had with a taxi. Bob decided he would send me with a hospital employee, and if the taxi driver, who is suing him, showed up with the witness, Bob would then come, too. The judge thought it was great they sent me, but the taxi driver didn't show. Since it is the third time, our lawyer said they would decide (the judge, he, and the other lawyer)—what a system! All of the lawyers walked in dressed in long sleeve shirts and ties. Then they had to put on long, black robes. All very impressive, especially if you consider the weather was over 100 degrees! Anyone and everyone who saw me standing amid the *Palace de Justice* came to my aide. Even the Chief of Kpodzi came to make sure it was just a small matter.

Love,

Shirley

May 8, 1989

Dear Mom,

God is in the business of answering prayer! First, I want to introduce Delali. She is our latest helper. She is learning to clean and iron to help Adzovi and I get through the summer. So far, she has worked out very well, and Adzovi is especially happy. Adzovi is so loyal. It has been a challenge to know how to help her without offending her at the same time. She is the trainer, and Delali was her choice.

Delali had a baby stillborn in our hospital, and it was then that she came to know Jesus. After telling us her testimony, Bob asked her if she remembered which person led her to understand the Scriptures. She said Justin, who is Adzovi's husband. It makes our morning Bible sharing and prayer time ever so beautiful.

Love,

Shirley

May 27, 1989

Dear Mom,

Thursday, Dal and Kay Washer stopped by the hospital en route to Kara where they planned to move while their son Denny and family take their furlough in the States.

Dal had had chest pain last week, and the pain was getting worse. Bob checked him out, and it looked like ordinary angina. The doctors asked Dal to delay his trip so they could be sure the medication was working. Dal wasn't that interested in staying, but he said he would consider it and was encouraged to rest at our house. So Dal was walking toward our house when he had a massive heart attack. Within a couple of minutes, the others had started CPR. Bob was called out of the OR in the middle of an operation, and they continued to work on Dal for an hour and half. Unfortunately, Dal passed away around noon.

That night I went down to Kpalimé to be with the family and help them plan the funeral. When I arrived, the yard was full of the blind students and their families. Kay calmly explained how the Lord had taken Dal home and how much each person there meant to her and Dal. Ron then challenged some of them to take his dad's place as an evangelist. The students sang a number of hymns and gave testimony of how Dal had influenced their lives. It was really precious.

Dal will be buried at the Blind Center and that has also been a tremendous testimony to the Togolese.

Love,

Shirley

June 4, 1989

Dear Mom,

The funeral for Dal Washer was such a testimony to so many people, both believers and unbelievers. Dal was a pioneer in missions to Africa, and so many people came to share how he impacted their lives.

Dal's family chose to bury him in Togo. The family did as much as they could Togolese style. We made the casket at HBB and took his body to Agou to freeze until all the family arrived. Then Bob and I went early and helped his sons prepare the body for viewing.

The wake the night before the funeral was so organized. I left about 10:30 p.m., but many stayed all night.

The procession from the church was at least a mile long of body-to-body people. Denny and Ron had invited all of their Zerma friends from Niger. Denny spoke in Zerma, and Ron translated from Zerma to French at the funeral. The gospel was once again shared, and Dal's life work was honored.

Love,

Shirley

June 6, 1989

Dear Mom,

This is a long, overdue letter. Life in Africa is supposed to be "slow and easy," but this month I served 72 extra meals at our table!

Since Dal died, Kay is not going to go to Kara as they had planned. Instead, our Pastor Paul has felt the burden to go to Kara to fill the gap for the next six months. What a joy to see him so sensitive to the Lord's leading. It will mean a lot of adjustments for us, so please pray with us about this situation. We are also in the middle of a building program at Kpodzi, and Pastor Paul's wife, Apolline, hasn't been in good health. God is able, and we trust Him to give wisdom and direction in this.

Our newest househelp, Delali, was beaming when we spent time in the Word and prayer on Monday morning. We have been praying for her grandmother who had surgery here last week. She has a bad cancer and needed a skin graft. Delali shared the gospel with her, and she accepted the Lord last Saturday. We got Delali a follow-up lesson so she can help her grandma grow in her new faith. The grandmother does not speak French or Ewe, so Delali will have to study one language and translate into another for her grandmother to understand.

Last Sunday, on my way to church, a lady ran in front of an approaching taxi. I stopped. The taxi driver took over, so I went on. On my way home after church, an approaching taxi was "all arms" flagging the taxi in front of me to stop. I ended up closest, and before I knew it, I had the same lady in my back seat. She was still close to hysteria. Through her tears, she explained that she needed to get to a village up the mountain close to the Ghana border. Her son had died from a motorcycle accident. This young man left eight small children. It was her second son to die in six months.

I picked up a lady, Beatrice, at the Tsiko church. She comforted and talked of God's love with the grieving woman. After we arrived at the destination, the lady would not let go of my hand. The body was being taken from a taxi, and the whole village was wailing. Beatrice stayed close, and I was so relieved to have her nearby.

The grieving lady said, "You need to tell us about this God who sent His Son to save us before it is too late. I've never heard."

Oh, Mom, did my heart weep! What a contrast to witness the sorrow of those without any hope with the homegoing of a precious saint like Dal, whose funeral is still fresh in my mind. Beatrice and I will visit the family this week and help where we can. We will present the gospel to the lady and those who will listen.

Love,

Shirley

July 21, 1989

Dear Mom,

I loved having our church family from Michigan visit! Yes, it did end up being a bit much, but we made it. I find myself working hard to stay positive because I feel so homesick since everyone left. I always was a homebody, wasn't

I, Mom? Didn't even go to camp too many times, and here I am in Africa! Miracles never cease! Luke often says, "We don't believe in miracles, we rely on them."

Pray that God would grant Bob and me special wisdom these days. This term, we are working with all first-term missionaries. As Bob works on hospital policies that have never been defined, he finds himself before the firing squad often! He tries to present solutions with the culture in mind, but principles of honesty and truth seem to be fading in our community. We have missionary men who don't want to preach, teach, or evangelize. Now tell me, how do you get churches planted? Families aren't even attending church regularly. Our Togolese brothers and sisters are beginning to wonder and be discouraged, which is just what the evil one would have. I'll say no more on this note, but do pray!

Must close. Talk again soon.

Love,

Shirley

August 30, 1989 Newsletter

Dear Mom,

"And they lived happily ever after." That is just what we would desire for all who enter Karolyn Kempton Memorial Christian Hospital, but it just isn't true.

Just this morning, Amen, six weeks old, was admitted into our ICU. She was in critical condition. Her mother and I prayed before I left for Bible school. When I returned, Guardian waited for me with a note: "Amen no longer suffers. She is with her Maker."

The Togolese custom for a child under three months of age is no casket and no service. However, we feel differently. Mr. Dzagli (along with a suburban full of others and the baby's body) accompanied me to Kpodzi. He had a graveside salvation message and gave an invitation for anyone listening to trust God. Three people wanted to learn more about our Lord. One of those men was Amen's uncle.

Then yesterday, another message arrived from Kpodzi: "It is the intention of this letter, Dr. and Mrs. Cropsey, to inform you that the infant of Mr. Laurent, Tonton, died yesterday evening in the Kpalimé hospital at the age of four years. He will be buried at 7:00, on August 29, in the morning. Please, Father, can you send us a pastor that can speak at the burial? Please inform the others."

Mr. Laurent led the slow procession down the street. He turned down a well-worn footpath which took us to a small hole dug at the back edge of the cemetery. He removed the cloth and placed the cardboard box into the hole along with its precious contents.

Tonton was in my Jr. church and so happy and quick to share his love for our Lord as only a four year old can. Many times Mr. Laurent asked us to speak to his wife concerning her need for salvation. As she sat in grief, I knelt before her. The stark reality of her need faced me. The compound was full of people, and our words were brief. Upon leaving with our group, a man came up to me and, in English, said, "Don't feel like your heart is being ripped out. God knows what He does." Then he disappeared.

The churchmen asked me to stay with them to represent Pastor-Doctor, their title for Bob. We went before the elders and the Chief, exchanged greetings, and sat. We were then led back to a room and given something to drink. Next, we found ourselves back at the compound of Mr. Laurent, where we sat for the subsequent hour sharing and singing with his wife and others.

Once again, the gospel in love was shared. Again, I was reminded that we serve a God of miracles and that God must do the calling and the changing of hearts. Only God can give this a bittersweet ending.

Please pray with us for Mrs. Laurent.

Love,

Shirley

October 12, 1989

Dear Mom,

I've just been working on Bible verses for Bible class. The boys are memorizing Luke 12:4-7. It says the following:

> Now I say to you, My friends, do not be afraid of those who kill the body, and after that have nothing more that they can do. But I will warn you whom to fear: fear the One who, after He has killed someone, has the power to throw that person into hell; yes, I tell you, fear Him! Are five sparrows not sold for two assaria? And yet not one of them has gone unnoticed in the sight of God. But even the hairs of your head are all counted. Do not fear; you are more valuable than a great number of sparrows.

The verses have been a blessing to meditate on realizing how much God truly cares for each of us. Just as you've had to put my care into His hands, I now have to do the same for you![1] I find I must do it daily, or I slip. It is so hard for me! And that is sin—what a patient and loving God we have.

Thank you for praying about our furlough plans. Yes, soon we will need to decide and make plans in a definite direction. Bob and the boys have some ideas of what they'd like to do. It will be Luke's last trip, so I am hoping it all works out.

Love you. Take care.

Love,

Shirley

December 1, 1989 Newsletter

Dear Mom,

As we begin to plan for our furlough year, we see that much has been accomplished this term. We, the humans, have not achieved it. It is only through God's strength and enablement!

As you know, Pastor Paul and Apolline moved to Kara to help shortly after the homegoing of Pastor Dal Washer. Mr. Divine Dzagli stepped in as interim pastor during their absence. Our people at Kpodzi anticipated their return this month. Our six-month loan was complete! However, Pastor Paul announced to the church Wednesday that he and his wife will remain in Kara to continue with the ministry among the Kabiyé people. We could be discouraged, but through this, we are reminded that God makes no mistakes.

Mr. Dzgali has been struggling with the thought of continuing at Kpodzi. Last night he, Mercy, and Bob spent time in prayer. During that time, Mr. Dzgali realized that God wants him not only to pastor the church at Kpodzi but put more time into it. The Lord has given Mr. Dzgali unique talents and insight into the people's needs. Bob, in faith, had already approached the medical committee and been granted any changes that may need to be made with the laboratory schedule to give Mr. Dzgali more time, as he is the lab director at the hospital. Praise the Lord!

The family is all well. Bob, like many men here, wears many hats. He is a father, husband, pastor, hospital administrator, director, medical committee chairman, teacher, etc. He is tired. Very unlike him, he says that he needs a break from it all. Each week we keep thinking maybe the next week will let up a bit, but each week (just as for you) is just as hectic. How concentrated we must be not to let the urgent steal from God's best for us.

Merry Christmas!

Love,

Shirley

February 4, 1990

Dear Mom,

Joshua is starting the painful task of finding new homes for his animals while we go on furlough. We took one cage and three rabbits to the village at the end of last week. He still has two more rabbits to sell and pigeons everywhere. He also wants to keep something to give the Andersons when they return to Togo. His little green parrot that he got when we went north was so friendly; sadly, it died.

The Egglestons are here as short-termers. He is a doctor, and they have four boys. That means I usually have at least seven boys around the house, sometimes nine. Doesn't add up? Well, the youngest Eggleston is just four years old and doesn't find our place interesting. The other two are Ron and Ryan Neufeld, long-time members of the activities here. And you thought kids on the mission field were isolated and disadvantaged? These boys have a pretty good team for just about any sport they take a liking for on any given day.

Mr. Dzagli is doing a great job at Kpodzi: He is diligent and faithful to the task. We had Sunday school classes last Sunday, the first since Pastor Paul left. I am teaching Mercy how to teach, and we are doing the ladies' class together. We are teaching on women of the Bible and started with Eve. Yesterday's lesson was about how women are equal in the sight of God and responsible to respond to God the same as their husbands.

Love you!

Love,

Shirley

March 4, 1990

Dear Mom,

By this time, you have probably gotten at least one suitcase from us and wonder what is going on. You will be getting another, and I will keep sending anything home via other travelers. It will just be that much less we will need to ship in the end! Thank you so much. I trust it will not be too much of an inconvenience for you.

It has taken a lot of prayer to get through these last few weeks. It seems that things at Kpodzi have been brewing for some time. Isn't God good to let the situation surface while we are still here?

One of our members took it upon himself to become the president of the church! He and several others also decided last Sunday they would ask Mr. Dzagli to leave the church and did so at a meeting called to deal with another problem.

Bob spent the rest of the day teaching on the biblical way to solve problems and the scriptural pattern for setting up a church. These are not new concepts but are new to these Togolese baby Christians.

Bob also spent yesterday afternoon trying to get the Chief to finish the church property papers. He has agreed to go to the government office on Thursday to have the land signed over, if he can find the papers.

Luke just got back from jogging, and it is time for me to get breakfast made so Bob can get out the door.

Love,

Shirley

May 1, 1990

Dear Mom,

This will be the last letter that you will receive from Togo this term, Lord willing! We are really in the last days of activity here. Even the dog, Comet, senses something will happen and acts like the world is folding in on him.

Yesterday we made history. We had our first Togo MK graduation. Luke and Lucinda, another MK, have completed their requirements for high school. Everyone was at the hospital for field council and joined in on the graduation.

Pray for Luke. He found out recently that his very good friend would be moving. We also had word from the school we thought the Lord would have him attend, and it will not be possible to schedule him as he would like this next year. God has something special for him, of that, we are confident.

Encouragement for the day: "Therefore if anyone is in Christ, this person is a new creation; the old things passed away; behold, new things have come." 2 Corinthians 5:17

Love,

Shirley

October 1, 1990 Newsletter

Dear Praying Friends,

Returning to America is always an adventure. All those things that we had taken for granted now seem exhilarating. For example, driving down a superhighway going from point A to point B without worry of striking a pedestrian, chicken, or goat. It is great to be back and see family and friends and rejoice with them in all that God has been doing in their lives and ours.

I have undergone extensive tests all summer and have been treated for filariasis, a microscopic parasite in the blood and lymphatic system.[2] This past weekend we traveled to Toronto where I underwent further evaluation by the chief of tropical medicine. He commented that my case was one of the most complex and challenging problems he had seen in recent years.

Would you pray with us that God will give the doctors wisdom to treat these serious problems? Please pray that God will give us the peace over our next steps and the ministry He would have us continue.

Love,

Shirley

April 17, 1991 Newsletter

Dear Mom,

It seems that God continues to place some great challenges on us so that He can demonstrate His all-sufficient grace and strength.

First of all, please pray about the upheavals happening in Togo. In the last several months, a number of political factions have demonstrated for a multi-party system. This past week, 27 of those people were found floating in a lagoon just outside of Lomé, the capitol. These political murders are the first sign of political unrest in decades. Please pray for the safety of all our Togolese brothers and sisters as well as missionaries in this time of uncertainty.

Thank you for praying for me. After several weeks of severe reaction to filaria treatment, I stopped the treatment and the test showed none of the filaria could be isolated. A week ago, I took my first dose of a new drug (Ivermectin) which was repeated again yesterday. The initial 48 hours after treatment are pretty rough, but I am feeling better today. A second drug has now been added which I will be taking for the next three weeks. Please pray that this will result in the destruction of these parasites and that healing will come.

Luke, our 17-year-old son, has seen God do special things in his life these past few months. In a miraculous sequence of events, God made it obvious that the Air Force Academy is his mission field for the next few years. Just two weeks ago, during the final hour of orientation at the Academy where all the prospective cadets and their parents were being briefed, there was a final announcement, "Would Mr. Luke Cropsey please report to the front of the auditorium after everyone is dismissed?"

Our hearts pounded. Did something come up that he didn't qualify after all? As we approached the front of the huge auditorium, the director of admissions warmly greeted us. He said he was so impressed with Luke's application papers that he personally wanted to meet him. "In fact," he went on to say, "You are known as the 'cobra killer' with the admissions committee." He then told us that he was a believer and that there were many Christian faculty members and cadets. He offered his assistance to Luke in any way possible while we were back in Africa. Glory be to God! In that moment, I remembered 1 Corinthians 2:9 that says the following:

Things which eye has not seen and ear has not heard,

And which have not entered the human heart,

All that God has prepared for those who love Him.

Love,

Shirley

August 8, 1991 Newsletter

Dear Praying Friends,

As I begin this letter and reflect back on all that has happened in the months since we last wrote, it has been nothing short of unreal. God has given us many mountain top experiences, and we have been in the valley on a number of occasions. We are continually learning from the Lord as Isaiah 55:8-9 says, " 'For My thoughts are not your thoughts, Nor are your ways My ways,' declares the LORD. 'For as the heavens are higher than the earth, So are My ways higher than your ways And My thoughts than your thoughts.' "

On Sunday, May 19, Keith and Sharon Talladay flew Bob and me to our Sunday meetings in their newly refurbished Cessna 210. Keith was a former F-4 pilot instructor with the Air Force, and he was reteaching Bob all he had forgotten since Bob's flying days in the Navy.

We all arrived home Monday and looked forward to another day of flying on Tuesday. After arriving home, Keith took the plane to a nearby airfield to refuel for our next trip. On his departure from refueling, he had engine failure and crash-landed in a field. As Bob assisted others on the operating team and then cared for him in the ICU, we prayed that God would spare Keith's life. But the Lord had other plans for Keith.

Keith was a wonderful friend, full of zeal for serving his Lord. He allowed us to use some buildings and his equipment to pack many containers headed for Togo. Keith's death left a large void in the lives of everyone who knew him. Over 900 friends and relatives came to say goodbye and to stand beside his beautiful family at his funeral.

Keith's wife, Sharon, reflected with Bob and me about the accident. We know it was only by the grace of God that we were not in the aircraft. It is a sobering thought of how close we came to death ourselves. We don't know or understand why God calls some of his choicest servants home and leaves us behind. But when we consider the fact that our lives are as vapor, no wonder God tells us to redeem the time. When I wake up to a new day, I am more appreciative and ask God to take me and use me like it may be my last.

As for our return to Togo, my health is the greatest concern. My doctors have been consulting with some of the world experts on the treatment of my problem with filaria. Ten days ago I started another treatment. Although the side effects are less, I still have a lot of symptoms. We praise the Lord for the people at church who have been helping with housework and providing meals. We pray that I will be cured of this tropical disease. My doctor says, however, that I may need several more courses of treatment.

Despite the treatment and delay in returning to Togo, I have learned a deeper and more dependent walk with the Lord. The Psalms have become meaningful in a new way. I thank God daily for his provisions in comfort and strength. Psalm 46:1-3 reminds me of the following:

> God is our refuge and strength,
>
> A very ready help in trouble.
>
> Therefore we will not fear, though the earth shakes
>
> And the mountains slip into the heart of the sea;
>
> Though its waters roar and foam,
>
> Though the mountains quake at its swelling pride. *Selah*

Love,

Shirley

December 1991 Newsletter

Dear Friends Around the World,

If you have been reading the newspaper, you have read about Togo. Unfortunately, the news is not good: an attempted coup with many people killed. The new prime minister was captured and held in the old president's palace to negotiate some type of coalition government. All telephone services and flights into Togo are suspended. Bob just talked to the American State Department and was told there is no active fighting and that Americans in the country are not in any immediate danger. Please pray with us for peace and a just political solution for our adopted country. Pray for the safety of all our friends. Pray that God will use this event to further the gospel in Togo.

Last time we saw my infectious disease doctor, just after Bob's safe return from Togo in October, we asked about a January return to Togo for the whole family. The doctor was open to the suggestion. Since then, I've completed a host of exams and tests. It is unlikely that I will undergo another treatment at this writing, but I still have more blood tests before the final decision.

Often as God leads us through tricky waters, it is less about us and more about accomplishing His will. Many of you remember when we shared about the death of our dear friend, Keith Talladay. The memorial gifts given in his honor have been used to purchase supplies to build a Bible Institute in Togo. Our loving home church family has committed themselves to provide the remainder of the financial need and send a team out next summer to complete the work. Kurt Sager has agreed to return to Togo to do the masonry task. We look forward to honoring Keith's life through this generous gift of so many!

Joyeaux Noel!

Love,

Shirley

January 31, 1992

Greetings from Togo!

It hardly seems possible that we left Michigan winter weather two weeks ago and are now in hot, dry harmattan season. The temperature here has been in the 100-degree range. The mountain out the side of the house is just an outline due to the thick dust in the air. Bob has been waking up in the middle of the night wheezing and needing his inhaler! I'm sorry for Bob, but it is a pleasant change for me.

The Broeckert family, who we have known since our time at language school, have been unable to return to their ministry outpost. So they remain here in Togo. Yes, that means there are a total of 13 people in our house. Bob and I have our bedroom with John on the floor; there are four boys in a room, four girls in another, and Hubert and Mary in the fourth bedroom. Our table sits 12 comfortably, so we get to snuggle up with 13 for meals! All is working out well. The kids are having a ball. They even manage to make washing dishes fun.

Adzovi started working for us last Tuesday, and it is so lovely to have her back. She and I work so well together that it seems like we never stopped! I can just about keep up with cooking these days and some unpacking while she does the laundry and cleaning of the rest of the house. All of the kids have jobs, so all chores get done one way or another. Haddessa, who is four years old, helped me make pies this morning. I'd forgotten the joy of what it's like to have such help.

There is a hot volleyball game getting organized. The kids need more players, so I'd better close. (To keep the kids happy, of course.) I enjoyed our visit.

Love,

Shirley

March 16, 1992

Dear Mom,

Some of the men from the mission have been invited to visit the interim prime minister of Togo tomorrow morning. Continue to pray for political stability here in the government. There continues to be an unhealthy undercurrent of activity. (It is best not to write to us about it.)

I took the plunge and swam in the pool last night for the first time. The moon was full, and it was so refreshing. Matt and Josh have the job of keeping the pool clean. They are both bored in their free time, so I am thankful for these types of chores.

It keeps trying to rain. The humidity is so high, and the temperature doesn't drop! I heard thunder this afternoon. It is cloudy but no rain yet. Maybe it doesn't rain because the motor for our windshield wipers doesn't work. Ha!

Take care. We love you.

Love,

Shirley

April 16, 1992

Dear Mom,

I can't think of a nicer thing to do than to sit down and have a visit with those I love on my birthday. Everyone has shown me so much love already that I can't imagine what else the day will bring.

I took directions, a book with great pictures, and my best French down to Sedro, the blacksmith, to have him make a large parrot cage for our living room. Joshua is getting two African grey birds. I'd like to have the birds inside to see if they will talk sooner. When they are outside, they don't hear enough.

Someone offered us two monkeys. I am passing on them. I just can't overcome my fear after seeing one attack our friend on our porch last term. Our German Shepherd Cuddles is growing fast and keeps us entertained. Oh, Joshua's anteater died. I can't imagine why because the ants are out in force right now. I was spring cleaning, so maybe the poison I set out got him as well. It was certainly an interesting animal to watch.

I gave haircuts this morning. The boys think I should do them just like the short-term beautician who was here. Their regular cut with her was a shave up the side coming to a *V* in the back. *Right.* Well, I did my best. Josh thinks he may need to wear a hat all weekend. The All-West African baseball tournament is in Lomé, and he doesn't have two days to wait until a bad haircut turns into a good one. Grandpa always said, "The only difference between a good haircut and a bad haircut is two days."

Bob and I were in Kpalimé for a prayer meeting last night and came back on the motorcycle. A full moon lit our path. I don't go out much at night, but this was a birthday treat. I saw all the cut-down trees. The Togolese are sacrificing the future on the altar of the immediate. It is so sad to see all the trees they've chopped down because of political unrest. The palms that grow out my back window have disappeared completely. I can see so far down the valley. It is rumored that in two weeks the moratorium to limit this type of behavior will be enforced. But I wonder, who will enforce it?

The morning is spent, and I need to work on other correspondence. Bob will come for lunch today, so I need to make the pizzas. The dough is rising, pies made, cabbage grated, and veggies have soaked, so I don't have too much time left in the kitchen. It is so hot here that I just drip whenever I have to cook.

Love,

Shirley

June 14, 1992

Dear Mom,

It doesn't seem that I've kept up with letters well, even with the slow incoming mail.

Mrs. Kwassi led the ladies' class this morning and did a super job. I remember when we prayed for nine months before our first lady came. Today there were 25 women. 15 of them could read! What an encouragement to me!

Before we returned to Togo, we faced insurmountable barriers. From most sides, the recommendation was "don't go back to the tropics." My pastor gave me counsel and suggested I study 1 Kings 19 with a special note of verses 11 and 12 where Elijah goes through the wind, earthquake, and fire. The end of verse 12 says, "and after the fire, a sound of a gentle blowing." It was the voice of God! Oh, to know the voice of God in our lives, despite the wind, earthquake, and fire of our circumstances. We decided to go back to Togo because God has not removed His call and burden to minister in Togo. There is much to be done yet, and we need your prayers.

We have been preparing for a group of 22 to come. I will share more about that later.

Co-laboring with you.

Love,

Shirley

June 23, 1992

Dear Mom,

I've been thinking of you so much this week. Maybe having friends here from home promotes it! All is going well. 22 people came, so we are busy. Kelli has been a lifesaver for me. I'll miss her when she leaves with the team.

Mail remains sporadic and slow, but all is quiet right now politically.

I had steroids to stop another allergic reaction this week. I began to taper the dose today and am doing fine. It's the same old thing—do you think it will ever stop?

Our love to all. Must close.

Love,

Shirley

July 4, 1992

Dear Mom,

It has been some time since I sat down to write everyone. This summer started with a bang, even before school got out!

I spent last week getting things cleaned, resorted, and repacked in readiness for the next team of professionals in August. It seems that it took more time to prepare for the last team of 22 than the amount of time they were here in Togo. It was a delight to have them, though! Considering the logistics of the work and ministry schedule, all went smoothly. For most of them, it was their first adventure being in a third-world country, actually living and being a part of people's lives, not just a tourist! Bob was thrilled that many of them took the time to be with him at the hospital or clinic. He enjoys sharing his work with others.

Of course, the dedication of the Bible Institute was the highlight of their time in Togo. Grandpa Talladay shared about our dear friend Keith who died when his airplane malfunctioned. Pastor Hall gave a challenge from the Word, sharing that just as these buildings were in memory of Keith, they stood to remind us of God's promises. Several of the current Bible Institute students also shared their testimonies.

Here's a fun tidbit. When the masons poured cement for the sports court, Bob had them fix my clothesline as well. Well, collapse! Yes, everyone thought it would be me, but instead, it was the clothesline on top of me after being filled with laundry for 28 people several days in a row. Both posts broke off at the grass line.

Bob just got home after being in the OR all morning. Yesterday he amputated both legs on a lady who had the fetish doctor in the village perform some sort of ceremony by slashing her feet and putting manure on them. Both feet became infected and gangrenous by the time she arrived here. Her life is still in the balance.

I had a visit from a special little guy last week. He brought gifts of fruit. The hospital treated him for a gunshot wound a little while back. The story is this: While he was visiting a friend, he saw the father beat his friend. The father raised a gun to shoot his son, and the boy stepped in to protect his friend. He lost his arm through the event. The injured boy and his family are Muslim. The boy has turned to Christ, and his family is listening. There seems to be no end to the opportunities to share Christ's love with others.

The field remains ripe for harvest, but the laborers are few!

Love,

Shirley

August 17, 1992

Greetings from Togo!

The weather has been just right. It is still the rainy season, so it is overcast and cool. But we saw the sun this morning.

Did I tell you that the Colonial team didn't arrive on their scheduled flight? We didn't know where they were for about 24 hours. After being at the airport all night Saturday, making frantic calls to the States and other places, we discovered they would arrive Monday. Then, just before they were to leave to go back home, we lost them again. How many times can you lose 11 people in five days?

On the last day, Joshua took them to see the waterfall near the Ghana border. This area could be described as "no man's land" because both Togo and Ghana debate about whose waterfall it is. While there, the Ghanian park reserve arrested them and took them to the Ghana jail.

Because they didn't have their passports, they didn't have any proof that they were visiting Togo. Josh finally talked them out of jail just when Bob and I were setting out to find them. (They were two and a half hours late to leave for Lomé and their plane home.)

Bob said, "Oh, they are probably in jail!" Sure enough, they were making more memories! I told them that I'd made just about enough memories for one week. Ha! All in all, it was a fantastic week. Full to overflowing. They worked round the clock to fulfill their mission in the five days they were here. Just this afternoon Bob operated under the new lights that were installed while the team was here.

I have been waiting for summer vacation to start, and now it is time for school to begin! I think that this summer has been the busiest since we came to Togo. Joshua and John have not been in their rooms since the first of May. Doing food and housing for all of the teams this summer has been a real challenge, along with being responsible for transportation, ministries, and work projects. God required much, but He also gave me the strength and grace to survive.

We also need you to double your prayers for protection. Last night someone attacked Guardian with a *coup coup*. He has several stitches but is okay. Guardian has been here since before the hospital and hardly ever leaves. I don't know any more details.

At present, because of my ongoing needs, we feel that next May, or so, we'll be coming back to the States for a while. Keep praying that we'll know His will in this matter. The boys, Matt and Josh, are anxious to return, too.

I really need to close and get some of these letters run off.

Love,

Shirley

September 5, 1992

Dear Mom,

I don't have much time before the power drops, but I wanted to send a quick note.

We are working on a checklist and evacuation procedure if the need arises. Presently, we feel in no immediate danger. There are roadblocks in every village making travel a nightmare some days. The dollar exchange continues to drop.

We were asked to seek counsel. Bob wonders if he needs to resign his position here. A lot of different things have happened for him to feel this is what God wants. This is NOT open information at this point. We haven't even talked with the boys.

All in all, I think it has taken Bob back to praying and seeking God's face and direction in it all.

Must close. Mom, are you still keeping my letters? Please do. One day they will serve as a reminder of all God has done.

Love,

Shirley

November 24, 1992

Dear Mom,

This paper contains some notes and thoughts of events from the last weeks. Don't let it dampen our celebration of who Christ is and what He means to each of us. He takes each of us "through the fire." There is no ditch too deep that God's love can't reach me and you. I have been meditating on Psalms 91 and 43 during this time. Here's the story:

On Monday, a couple who was helping short-term came with me to Adeta to see if there was market. With all the political strife, it's hard to know day to day what to expect. We took the small, red car and drove back to a deserted market area. Just behind the post office, there was some selling and all seemed peaceful. So we locked the car and strolled around. The man with us, I'll call him B, had his video camera, but I'd advised him not to take photos. After making a few purchases, with many explanations of sights, sounds, and smells, a faint murmur floated past and people started to run.

I told the couple that I didn't know what the problem was, but we needed to leave quickly. As we came up an incline, a man from the market said,

"Oh don't go. It is nothing," but God prompted me to continue toward the car. I unlocked all the doors. The lady and I were in the car when B, unknown to me, made a sweep of the market with his camera. Suddenly, the mass of people were now running at us!

There was just enough time to say, "Lock the doors!" The men from the market were hollering at us. B got in the car but so did another guy who started beating him and grabbing his neck. The next thing I knew, someone put a block in front of our rear wheel.

By then, I knew we were in trouble. At training, we were given a lecture on terrorists, and the expert said to use your car as your weapon. In a split second, after asking for God's help, I drove over the block and took off. Meanwhile, B is getting strangled in the backseat, and we don't know why!

Crossing the main road, I came to a spot where there was only gravel. The pavement had long ago washed away. The man who was struggling with B reached up, grabbed at me, and pulled the emergency brake, which threw the car sideways. We were stopped crosswise in the road beside the empty taxi stands. The motioned whipped my head around, and I saw the camera lying on the floor.

Not knowing why we were being stormed, I told B to throw his camera out the open door. In a split second, the mob was upon us again, but B pushed the man out of the car as the man reached for the camera on the ground.

Another guy was trying to talk to me at the window. He knew me and was trying to help. But the mob was uncontrollable even though they now had B's camera.

By now, the mob is on the road pounding the windshield, trying to pry open the doors, throwing dirt and gravel. The number of them was growing. The man who knew me said, "Just go!"

With my foot on the accelerator, we headed down the hill and over the bridge. Someone threw a stone, and it came through the back window. The window shattered as we bounced over the huge holes in the road.

Looking in the rearview mirror, I saw that the road was full of people.

I knew that the rule of thumb is to get out and stop at the next village. Thank the Lord that the Tsiko Chief was home. He took a quick look and let me keep going to Bob. He knows us. I was pretty sure if the mob caught up to us in his village, he'd protect me.

Mom, it all happened so fast. I didn't do anything different than I've done most Mondays since coming here. Everything is still a fog.

B had lots of glass on him and a badly scratched neck. I had several bruises and abrasions, but the lady was unharmed. We definitely sacrificed the car. It has three major dents, a warped door frame, no back window or windshield wipers. A lot of the reflectors were torn off. You get the idea.

It was only later that we started to put the pieces together.

Depending on what report you believe, the unrest started a year ago when Kabiyé people were killed in the village of Bodji. Word is that now Adeta (which is an Ewe village) will be wiped out, and "they" are just waiting for the opportunity. Chiefs have set up traps to protect their villages. The morning of our incident, Chiefs told their warriors to beat and kill anyone with a camera. They are afraid of the strike. If someone gets a photo and identifies them in the market, then a hit man will be sent. Turns out what happened to us was all just a very bad mistake. The short-term couple had just arrived and no one knew them. The man, B, didn't listen to my instructions and took out his camera. And because of that, we were later told the mob had meant to kill us.

I, along with Bob and a couple others from the hospital, spent a couple of hours with the Chiefs (five in all). They apologized. We still don't have the camera. They asked us to buy two bottles of gin and give them money in exchange for the camera. Of course, there is no way they can fix my car. Praise the Lord, though! We had several opportunities to share our testimony with them and the real reason that keeps us here: God's love for them. (No, we didn't buy gin in exchange for the camera. Instead we offered Bibles and our friendship.)

Sitting at the dinner table that night, one of the boys asked Bob how long we were going to stay in Togo. "Until one of us gets killed?" he asked.

With sad eyes, Bob responded with a question, "How long did Jesus stay on earth to save us?"

I was so ashamed of my thoughts of wanting to leave Togo!

We are at level two of our evacuation plan: bags packed and in the car, no one leaves the compound without a Togolese companion, and no cameras in sight!

I made muffins and bread to send to each Chief this morning. One of our missionaries said to me, "How can you be nice to them after all of this?" It is difficult. I need courage and love only God can give. I'm left with a caution light, but God's peace does pass all understanding.

Our Togolese friends came to express their grief and condolences that such an atrocity could occur here and to me. Mama Guardian came tonight with gifts and words of encouragement.

The strike continues. We remain very concerned about the policy to kill first and then ask questions. In a village of 6,000 people, how many really know us? All *yovos* look alike. Don't ask me to identify individuals in the mob either!

Thanksgiving preparations continue as planned.

The hospital census is low with no major surgery cases. We are down to skeleton staff. How long can we go like this before we need to just close?

Love,

Shirley

December 8, 1992

Dear Mom,

The strike continues into its fourth week. Things are not improving. The people refused to accept the negotiations made by the president and the prime minister. There are continued reports of scattered shootings.

There is a meeting this morning with the hospital staff to decide what our next move needs to be. Presently, the hospital is closed until the strike ends. How we need God's wisdom!

Bob and I have visited all of our employees in their homes since the hospital is closed. Reports say food prices have risen terribly, but it is still available if you know where to look. Only the reckless taxi drivers brave the roads. They charge outrageous prices. Roadblocks are scattered. Evangelistic meetings were canceled this week at Zomayi because of the tense activity in Kpalimé.

John has been pushing that we comply with the strike to the fullest and not have school. I tried to explain to him that it would only mean school into the summer when I know he will not want to study.

The Chiefs all came to express their regrets again for the mob scene and damage done at the market several weeks ago. They listened to God's love for each of them. We continue to pray it will be an open door to a Chiefs' Bible study. They sent word that they are waiting to receive the promised Bibles.

You know Bob would not buy them gin.

Love,
Shirley

December 17, 1992

Dear Mom,

The strike continues and the atmosphere remains characteristic of static electricity! I cannot get a good handle on where or when the tide will change. Even our people have very mixed feelings. The rumor was last week that Adeta would be leveled and burned! Several of our employees moved their families to the hospital at night. The radio says that all negotiations have stopped because the opposition refused the offer made by the prime minister and the president. It also said that the hospital closed because we ran out of medications, which was not the case at all. So much for freedom of the press!

Bob and I continue to visit our employees in their homes. We take popcorn and flavored drinks, and you would think we were giving them a Thanksgiving feast! It makes me so aware of how far apart our worlds are. Just another reminder that we can never outgive the Lord.

All around us we see the reality of how fragile life is. We have become dependent on God to supply our every need, and He has not let us down. One example of God's provision is the fact that a fellow came up to Bob when he was last in Adeta and said he was going to find him a back window for our car. Everything is closed, so it is impossible to get the car repairs done. Several days later, the man came with a window that he had somehow gotten from Ghana! Actually, he had the whole back of a car and told Bob where to take it and have it put in for 1,000 CFA. I guess to really understand the miracle of this story, you'd have to understand what we work with all of the time trying to get things done! Anyway, the window is fixed! And it was done in 15 minutes for 1,000 CFA! Amazing!

I am still receiving condolences for the actions of the mob, and it has been a great opportunity to give glory to our Lord for His protection. I've gotten so many gifts of bananas that we have been making bread all day!

Love,

Shirley

January 28, 1993 Newsletter

Dear Mom,

What is God doing since the riot in Adeta when I was mobbed? After we went and appeared before the Chiefs, we were asked to give several gifts in exchange for the camera. Instead of the gin asked for, Bob offered to give them Bibles. After a series of culturally polite meetings, Bob and Mr. Gingrich, who is a fellow short-term missionary, went to present the Bibles to the men. They had the opportunity to share with them that if they truly wanted to understand the Bible, they needed to have a spiritual understanding which comes only as a result of a personal relationship with God. Bob shared his testimony and presented God's desire for each of them to accept His plan of salvation.

Praise the Lord with us! At the first Sunday Bible study, four of the Chiefs prayed to receive Christ as Lord and Savior. These men have been faithful to study God's Word, do their lessons each week, and share their faith with family, friends, and associates. The group has grown, and last week there were 13 people. As God works in hearts, pray that we would continue to see fruit—may it be fruit that will remain! I thank God for a godly husband who helped us work through our human reactions to this difficult situation. God used it for His glory!

Love,

Shirley

March 1, 1993

Dear Mom,

It has been a rather uneventful day for me. I can take a couple more like this any time! Poor Bob, though, stayed overnight in Lomé to get money, gas, groceries, and our tickets for London. (In London, I have an appointment at the Tropical Disease Hospital.)

It is HOT. Harmattan has left, but the rains are not very regular yet. It is so humid! The temperatures are well over 100 degrees these days.

The market is picking up. The president called off the strike, but he is not the one who called it so there seems to be some debate. There are no negotiations going on presently. The opposition fled to France as best as we know. Mr. Nanda, who is a diamond dealer and exchanges our money, left last week too. His close friend and bodyguard was murdered at 8 a.m. in his office.

He said he just had to get out to think all of this out before he decides what he needs to do. It makes one more thing difficult for us. The banks haven't been open since the strike started! Bob hoped we could get our London tickets with our credit card because I paid everybody at the end of the month, and we are out of cash!

We ran into Shela, the nurse for the Peace Corps, at the airport last night. She was helping folks get out of Togo and was surprised that we had anyone coming in. She told Bob to go to the embassy and ask for help getting money. "After all," she said, "Remind them that you are their lifeline if they need medical help." She commented that she will have to think about a move, too, if the embassy will not help.

I need to close and get supper ready. Take care.

Love,

Shirley

April 1993 Newsletter

Dear Mom,

Growing, growing, growing! That could accurately describe the boys, the Chiefs' Bible study, the ladies' Kpodzi and Zomayi Bible study, our Kpodzi chapel, and the frequency of tropical downpours. Even the village market seems to be expanding each week. The strike continues, but the hospital workload has become as busy as ever. Bob spent several hours in the OR yesterday working on a 14-year-old boy who was accidentally shot in the head at the border by a soldier. Praise the Lord he is talking today; although, he is unable to move his right arm.

Many of you prayed for us during our recent business/medical trip to London. I was admitted to the Tropical Disease Hospital in London on March 31. I again went through a battery of tests, and we are still waiting to hear the doctor's recommendations. His initial thought was that there is another parasite that we have not yet treated causing at least some of my symptoms.

During the past few years, we have prayed that God would provide a special medical resource person at ABWE headquarters to help us and other ABWE hospitals find new personnel for critically understaffed medical ministries worldwide. As we shared with you while we were home, we felt the unrelenting, vicious attacks of Satan, specifically against our medical works. Over the years, we have lost many of our choicest medical personnel.

Have you ever discovered that praying can be dangerous because sometimes God asks you to be the answer to your own prayer? During our time in London, ABWE directors asked Bob to prayerfully consider becoming the new International Director of Medical Missions with the primary goal of enlisting desperately needed medical ambassadors for our medical outposts and then helping with the needs of hospitals. And not unlike Moses, we wondered why us and not someone else. But God has continued to confirm to us that He would have us step out in faith into these completely uncharted waters for both us and ABWE. How we need your prayers as we begin making plans for this exciting, and at the same time, intimidating new ministry in July.

We need God's strength and grace to take us through these days of shifting responsibilities, covering ministries, sorting, selling, and packing. Our farewells will be precious and sweet as we recall His blessings on this ministry. As we reflect on our last ten years in Togo, you have been an important part of our team as you have faithfully prayed and supported us in so many ways over the years. Despite our weaknesses, failures, and inabilities, we cry, "TO GOD BE THE GLORY! GREAT THINGS HE HAS DONE."

Love,

Shirley

May 20, 1993

Dear Mom,

The strike continues. All is quiet—feels sort of like "the calm before the storm." The elections have been canceled again. They are supposed to be June 20. That is better for us because it was originally scheduled for June 10, too close to our departure date.

Bob made all the arrangements for our pick up in Chicago.

We are packing the container today and tomorrow. There is too much to fit on it so it will be interesting. I'm still trying to keep up with everything. This afternoon I'll drive back to the hospital to do a staff ladies' meeting.

Tsiko, Joshua's team, won the soccer game, so they will play in the final game. Josh stayed with the team on Saturday night. He said they all got up every two hours to pray! It was a real cultural experience for him. They vote on who will play, so he was honored to be chosen. He played the whole first half. It got pretty wild at the end, so once again we left in haste. I'm glad for Joshua that his team won, but I have a knot in my stomach anytime I'm in a rowdy crowd.

Our days are really packed until we leave. Adzovi is here. This place is a mess! Need to close this and rearrange things so I can stand it for a couple more weeks.

I love you and can't wait to see you soon!

Love,

Shirley

October 1993 Newsletter

Dear Mom,

So long, FAREWELL . . . agonizing words that missionaries learn are to be a part of their life. But this time, it was especially humbling and difficult as we said our last goodbyes to missionary colleagues and dear Togolese brothers and sisters in Christ who showered their love on us in so many ways. It was truly a wonderful reminder of all that God had accomplished over the past ten years in and through His work in Togo. Our last days in Togo left us with many precious memories. Another very bittersweet time in our lives.

Our first goodbye was to Matt as he left us in March after finishing high school. All of his missionary aunts and uncles came to a special open house to wish him God's best. His entire basketball team gave him a very special farewell and thanked him for being their instructor and coach. He is now enjoying his freshman year studying missionary aviation at Bob Jones University. He reports that he is doing exceptionally well in all of his classes. A little special treat is that one of his roommates is his cousin from France, Andrew.

Two weeks before our departure, we celebrated one of the great milestones of our missionary career. We commissioned the *Eglise Baptiste Bibilique de Kpodzi* into independence, which I have so often referred to in my letters simply as "the church at Kpodzi." So many came to celebrate that we held an all-afternoon celebration. The village elders were also present and my good friend the Chief gave the church a charge of encouragement. As a medical missionary family first arriving in Togo, we never dreamed that God would give us the responsibility of planting a church. What a tremendous joy; we give all the credit to the Lord and His use of faithful, godly Togolese men and women who gave so generously of their time and talent, as well as abundant good advice and help from missionary colleagues over the years. And, of course, your prayers.

During our last week in Togo, we visited for the last time the home of many of our Togolese and missionary friends. Our entire Togo field council gave us a delightful farewell with laughter and tears. The medical staff and employees also gave us a signed group photo that we will forever cherish. On our last

Sunday, we had a Bible study in Adeta with the Chiefs and everyone they invited. It was a wonderful three-hour conclusion in the blazing hot sun. In that Bible study, the Chief's college-age son and daughter accepted Christ as their Savior. The Chief was overjoyed!

WELCOME TO THE USA greeted us as we passed through customs in Chicago and began our reverse culture shock of returning to the land of our beginnings. God placed on our hearts a new assignment, although we don't know how He is going to work out all the details. In Acts 20, Paul recounts a similar episode in his life as he concludes his third missionary journey. He stands on the Mediterranean Sea shore saying his last goodbyes to a group of friends. Several of them wept freely, realizing they would never see him again. After taking a long last look into their eyes, he told them that in obedience to the Holy Spirit, he was going back home to Jerusalem, not knowing the things that would happen to him there.

God directed us back to the USA at this particular time with the primary mission of enlisting and helping to train medical ambassadors. Over the past few years, God has stirred our hearts with the great personnel needs in all of our ABWE medical outposts worldwide. There is, also, an enormous need for establishing other new medical outposts as part of our church planting endeavors.

Most of our medical outposts are literally hanging on by their fingernails until reinforcements arrive. The problem is that there are few reinforcements on the horizon. Only a few brave souls are enlisting as medical ambassadors.

Along with visiting our supporting churches and speaking in mission conferences, we will focus on enlisting future medical ambassadors and encouraging them in their various stages of preparation. There are many in our Christian colleges and universities, medical schools, and residency programs who have been burdened. I also believe there remain many others, including those already in practice, whom God will burden and call as they are confronted with the great need and hear about the great impacts that they can have in medical evangelism.

It happens to all of us who listen to the still, small voice of God . . . going, yet not really knowing. As He leads us along, step by step, in a certain direction it often starts out illogical. So, like many who have gone before us, we step out in obedience. We pack our bags, bid our farewells, and strike out for a future that is as uncertain as it is clear! Wow, it sure feels shaky, but the quiet peace of God reassures us that He directs us. We pray that God will lead scores of others down this exciting path of faith and trust.

After leaving our home in Africa, we moved nine times before getting into the new home we now enjoy. It is a thrill to see God answer prayer and begin to use this home as a tool in our new ministry of service. We are already praising the Lord for the number of people God has given us who have a sincere interest in medical missions.

Perhaps you are experiencing the prompting of God to loosen your tent pegs, suggesting it's time for a change. Remember, God calls us here on planet Earth. So go ahead and take that big step of faith. Be ready to go whenever and wherever He leads. A decision you will never regret!

TO GOD BE THE GLORY!

Love,

Shirley

The Rest of the Story . . .

For years, Bob recruited doctors and nurses for the mission field. He made trips to Togo and other medical mission fields around the world, and he attended medical conferences and schools within the United States to speak to students in various stages of their training. With the help of generous donors and a hardworking team, a second ABWE hospital was built in northern Togo. Bob, along with others passionate about the work, created a network of doctors, medical personnel, and donors from all around the world called Medical Friends of Togo in which they share needs specific to the ABWE hospitals in Togo. Even with his retirement from ABWE, Bob shares the gospel and the mission field with anyone who will listen.

In the late 1990s, during a doctor shortage at HBB, Bob and I, empty-nesters at the time, returned to Togo to serve. During those five years, even though it had been years since my time as a nurse, I agreed to learn and work as a circulating nurse and give anesthesia in the OR. It had always been Bob's dream for us to work together in the OR.

Later, when we were back in the U.S., we built a home in Ypsilanti, Michigan, with a space specifically for my mom. She lived with us until her 90s. I thank the Lord for a godly, wise mother who faithfully prayed for me and saved my Togo letters. It was a profound experience to be a part of her life both as a child and as a friend.

As I look back on my life, I can see how God prepared me for Togo. But just because we left the medical mission field did not mean my job was over.

Shortly after our return from Togo, a doctor contacted me and asked if I would sponsor a Bible study for residents' wives through Side by Side, a ministry under the Christian Medical and Dental Association (CMDA). Through the years, I have been able to mentor and sit alongside other medical professional wives.

I occasionally speak in churches and other venues about my time in Togo and what God has taught me through the years, and for many years I taught God's plan in the two and three-year-old Puggles classroom, the youngest group of Awana Bible study participants.

I've had the opportunity to host many friends and family through the years in our home, and I continue my ministry of correspondence to friends around the world. (But through a faster mode—the internet!)

My mom passed away in 2020, but I cherish the godly heritage and the encouragement she gave to me to follow God's leading. When I was growing up, much emphasis was on giving honor to parents and grandparents as found in Exodus 20:12, "Honor your father and your mother, so that your days may be prolonged on the land which the LORD your God gives you." These verses shouldn't be dismissed, but when I was younger, I didn't understand how deep God's plan and love for us runs.

In Psalm 25 God teaches us about both sin and righteousness, and He shares that the man who chooses to fear the Lord and walk in His ways will be prosperous. In verse 13*b* it says, "His descendants will inherit the land." Much of the Old Testament, when speaking about inheritance, talks about land, but there are also verses that infer it can be spiritual blessings: "Blessed be the God and Father of our Lord Jesus Christ, who has blessed us with every spiritual blessing in the heavenly places in Christ. " (Ephesians 1:3)

I was blessed with a mom and grandma who were willing to share with me on a spiritual level and that to me was much more precious than any earthly inheritance! Grandma shared God's Word and His faithfulness to her, and my mom shared it often through her talks with her grandkids. Psalm 71:18 says the following:

And even when I am old and gray,

God, do not abandon me,

Until I declare Your strength to this generation,

Your power to all who are to come.

At the writing of this book, Bob and I are blessed with 13 grandchildren. My prayer is that my obedience will continue to encourage others, especially my grandchildren. May my life be a spiritual heritage to you and may these letters encourage you to pursue God no matter what life brings.

The Gift

You may have just finished reading this book and have no idea why someone would be so sad to know that people passed into eternity without knowing Jesus personally. A holy God made a way for each of us through His Son to be with HIM. He presents it as a gift; it is not earned or deserved or forced on us. Ephesians 2:8-9 says, "For by grace you have been saved through faith; and this is not of yourselves, it is the gift of God; not a result of works, so that no one may boast."

Receiving this gift is a personal choice. To make the gift yours, you must accept it. John 3:16 says, "For God so loved the world, that He gave His only Son, so that everyone who believes in Him will not perish, but have eternal life." God sent His only Son, "who knew no sin" (2 Corinthians 5:21), to die on a cross to pay the price for our sin. Isaiah 53:6 says, "All of us, like sheep, have gone astray, Each of us has turned to his own way; But the LORD has caused the wrongdoing of us all To fall all on Him."

Would you like to receive this gift? Acts 16:31 says, "Believe in the Lord Jesus, and you will be saved." It means that you transfer your trust from what you have been doing to what Christ has done for you on the cross. Accept God's plan and receive Jesus Christ as Lord. Some have related it to driving a car: Just give Him the "driver's seat" and "controls" of your life, not the "back seat."

By faith, believe and ask Jesus to forgive you of your sins and become LORD of your life!

Letters from the Cropsey Sons

John Cropsey, youngest son of Bob and Shirley Cropsey

John married his high school sweetheart, Jessica, while still an undergrad. He received his bachelor's and medical degrees from the University of Michigan, and Jessica received her bachelor's and master's degree from Eastern Michigan University while also working to put John through medical school. They continued to pursue God's calling on their lives to be missionaries and moved to Philadelphia for John's residency in ophthalmology at Wills Eye Hospital. They have three children: Elise, Micah, and Sam. After residency, they spent 14 years as part of a "home-grown" medical missionary team from Ann Arbor called the "McCropders" serving in Kenya, France, and Burundi, focusing on medical education and discipleship with Serge. It grew from a motley crew of three couples to a large team of over 50 people. They have recently transitioned to a new role with Serge and will be focused on developing an ophthalmology residency program in Kigali, Rwanda, as well as being a regional resource for eye care in the Great Lakes region of Central Africa.

Mom: The Investor

Mom was pretty sick when I was just a little guy in Québec from the ages of two to four years old. Honestly, I don't remember those days much, just giant piles of snow in the parking lot. Rumor has it that I would quietly sit by Mom's bed and look at my Richard Scarry's *Goldbug* book for hours at a time. Apparently, God was honing a one-track mind that allowed me to study for hours on end to get through university and medical school. I'm pretty sure Mom's constant prayers and God's sense of humor had more to do with any success than *Goldbug* in the final analysis, but I like to think it played some kind of formative role.

When we arrived in Africa to a tropical paradise, Mom wisely released us four boys to the wild, and we loved it. Mom had many health battles that I was unaware of at that age. She was always putting us first and never complained about the challenges God allowed to come into her life. With Dad gone at the hospital often day and night, I really have no idea how she didn't go crazy raising us four "high energy" boys without losing it. But don't feel too bad for her; she prayed that God would give her boys to raise. That wouldn't be the last of her prayers to be answered in life, but she may have regretted praying that specific one at times.

Mom didn't just gift me with *Goldbug*. She taught me kindergarten for lack of other options. We joke to this day that I can't recite the alphabet or spell for my life because of that year, but honestly, I think I come by it genetically. Mom isn't the best speller either.

While we loved swinging from vines, riding motorcycles, and going on countless adventures as young boys, some of my most formative times as a young man came when I would plop down next to Mom in bed when she was too sick to get up. We'd talk about anything and everything from the mundane to the profound. We'd talk about life's struggles, God, grace, and the occasional girl. Mom always made time to listen and spend time with me. We had a bedside chat most afternoons or evenings as I got older.

Seeing Mom so sick was tough, and I would worry about losing her. When we had to leave Togo because things were getting so bad, I remember hearing Mom cough for hours on end to the point where she would gag uncontrollably in the bathroom. Her parasites would become active at night and irritate her airways. It weighed on me as a teenager, but Mom had such a God-oriented perspective that it kept me from becoming bitter. Mom's faith helped me trust God rather than become disillusioned.

One of the things that amazes me about Mom is that she doesn't wallow in self-pity, but instead, she redeems the time even when she is stuck in bed sick. I'm such a sissy when I get sick that I'm pretty much good for nothing. Not Mom! She prays, she digs into God's Word, she listens to others, and she writes letters and endless notes of encouragement to people all over the world. When I look at all the struggles God has allowed me to go through, be it a severe depression during my medical internship or political turmoil in Africa, I know the prayers of Mom (and many others) have sustained me, brought about miraculous healing, and provided divine protection for our family.

Mom, I couldn't ask for a more amazing person to have raised me. Thank you for bringing so much joy into our lives despite all of the suffering. I look forward to the day when God will redeem every pain, ache, and tear in your life to reveal something most unimaginably beautiful. With all of the lives you have touched on this earth, I think we have already been given a foretaste of what that will look like.

Luke Cropsey, eldest son of Bob and Shirley Cropsey

Luke left the house at 17 years old with a permission slip from his mom to attend the Air Force Academy. He's been wearing the uniform ever since and is now a Brigadier General. He and his wife Heather celebrated their 25th wedding anniversary this past year, and they have four kids who love the Lord: Maegan, Molly, Ethan, and Emily. They have had the privilege of carrying the gospel message to the military community for the past 30 years and have seen the Lord's faithfulness across multiple states, time zones, and countries.

My Praying, Patient, Encouraging Mom

I was old enough to remember when Mom came down with her original bout of mononucleosis and encephalitis while we were up in Québec in language school, prior to leaving for Togo.

It's funny that the memory that sticks in John's head are piles of snow because I have the same recollection. We lived in a big apartment building with a big parking lot. The snow plow piled all of the snow up at the end of the parking lot, so by the middle of winter, we had a huge pile of snow to play on.

The other thing I remember about our time in Québec is Dad stepping up to the plate while Mom was sick and confined to bed. Prior to that, it was almost all Mom when it came to meals, laundry, house cleaning, well, you name it! And even when Dad was in charge, we all survived!

While John was reading *Goldbug* books, the rest of us boys were all in school of one sort or another. Matt and I were put into a French-speaking Catholic school, and I think Josh was in a bilingual kindergarten. My strongest recollections from that time was Mom's bedroom needing to be dark and quiet. I was eight and nine years old at the time, so hard to say how accurate that impression is, but that's what sticks with me for some reason. We spent an extra year in Québec (two years total) to give Mom a chance to recover more fully before we left for Togo.

From that point forward, I don't think Mom's health ever fully recovered. She had better years than others, and I remember our first term out in Togo seemed relatively "normal" from that perspective, but I'm not sure that wasn't as much a result of having just grown used to the fact that Mom was sick, versus her having recovered from her previous ailments.

Our second term in Togo was when I remember her being really sick with filaria. One memory that stands out in stark relief from that time was a trip that I got to take with another missionary family, the Bronsons, who were with Wycliff Bible translators. Their son Nate was about my age, and they were headed up to Kara on the north end of Togo for a few weeks and invited me to go with them. We had an ABWE family up there as well, Denny and Diane Washer. One day after I had been up there for about ten days, Uncle Denny showed up at the guest house where we were staying. He said Mom was really sick, and he needed to drive me back to the hospital right away. That was the longest eight-hour drive of my life, wondering if Mom was going to make it. Dad flew back to the States with her the next day and left us with one of the single missionary guys for the next two weeks.

We could write an entire book on our exploits with Neil while Mom and Dad were back in the States, but I think it was really a gift of grace from the Lord because Neil did so many crazy things with us that we didn't really have time to dwell on how sick Mom was.

In addition to John's comments, I think of three things that have always stood out to me about how Mom has handled the poor health trials the Lord has allowed into her life. First, like John said, Mom has never grown bitter over her lack of health but has instead used it as a constant testimony to proclaim God's love and compassion to countless people that have had the benefit of interacting with her, both from a medical perspective as well as in a broader ministry setting. Her trust in God's sovereignty and His love in her life, even after years of medical ailments, put practical context around what is often dry theology for most of us. As John said, she hasn't allowed her health to be an excuse when it comes to serving the Lord, and she has been an inspiration to me personally on multiple occasions when it comes to the power of prayer and what the Lord can do in and through someone who faithfully pursues the throne of grace on behalf of others.

There is no question in my mind that the blessings in my life are in large measure a direct reflection of Mom's ministry of prayer for us when she is flat on her back in bed, too wiped out to do anything else.

Second, her patience and forbearance stand out to me in a big way. She is a modern Job in my mind, and she has the patience of Job in a very literal sense that transcends the cliché in a way that only someone who has suffered and endured and still falls back on the fundamental certainty of God's goodness and compassion toward them can really know and understand. It would be hard to capture all of the ways this comes out in everyday interactions with her, but you can see it everywhere if you hang out with her for any length of time. Her patience with a medical profession that seems to guess at a treatment regime of trial and error (I'm speaking as someone looking at this from the outside-in with no medical training) has always been mind-boggling to me.

And trying to contain my dad puts Mom at a whole different level all by itself! I think I can literally count on one hand the times I've seen her "lose" her patience, and there have been plenty of occasions where it would have been more than understandable. It also comes out in spades when she is interacting with kids. I've never seen her get frustrated with them. She patiently directs their behavior in the right direction, and my own kids would be front and center in this discussion!

Third, I think of how she encourages others. In the midst of her own physical suffering, Mom is the most consistent note writer of anyone I know. All of us can speak to the myriad of times when an email, notecard, or letter has shown up from Mom to thank us for something, let us know she was thinking and praying for us, or giving us an update on how things were going on the home front. She has always been "other" oriented in the things she does. Getting her to give you the "real story" on how she is doing personally has always been a challenge. The Apostle Paul talks about the power of a thankful heart in fighting against heresy and corruption in the church when he wrote to the Colossians, and I think the way Mom is "thankful" for the people in her life comes out as encouragement for them. But I think it is also one of the things the Lord has used to protect the grace and loving kindness in my Mom's own life. It's counterintuitive in many ways, but I think Mom's focus on others is a gift the Lord gives back to her as much as it is an encouragement to the person Mom is ministering to. It is an example I strive to emulate every day as I engage with a world in desperate need of a loving Savior.

Love you, Mom! There isn't a day that goes by that I don't thank God for the blessing of the godly heritage He gave the four of us boys growing up the way we did in a house that exemplified what the love of Jesus looks like on a daily basis.

Josh Cropsey, Third son of Bob and Shirley Cropsey

Josh headed off to Bible college in 1995, finished his Master of Divinity in 2001, and completed his Master of Education in 2016. Josh and Nannette have been married for almost 20 years and have three children: Jackson, Keziah, and Selah.

Mom the Brave

Many of my memories are very similar to my brothers' memories. I wish I could remember more from our time in Canada. I was quite young at the time. I do remember going to a kindergarten that was English part of the day and French part of the day. I also remember strange things like Matt flipping over his handlebars on a bike, Matt hitting me in the face with a hockey stick, my refusal to do the chicken dance at school because it wasn't "godly," lots and lots of snow, and touring the old fort in Québec. I remember loading up the car and driving to Canada. I also remember going back a second year due to Mom's sickness.

During our time in Togo, I remember Mom being sick for long stretches of time. Like John, I have very fond memories of lying next to Mom on the big water bed that was still cool after the generator went off at night. Mom used to read us books and just talk with us.

We had some great talks, Mom! You were always there to listen, and you loved us well. I am so grateful that you decided to be a stay-at-home mom and raise us boys. I know it was hard work!

One of my favorite memories of Mom was when another missionary confiscated our BB guns and marched us down to the house to talk with Mom. It was a long and stern lecture all the way home. The lady handed our guns to Mom and left. Mom smiled and told us to stay away from the lady and promptly handed our guns back! Again, Matt was with me.

Perhaps the thing that I'm most grateful to Mom for was being sensitive enough to know when we needed to talk. I will never forget the night that Mom sat next to my bed and shared how much Jesus loved me, and I decided to give my life to Jesus. I remember having this overwhelming sense of joy and peace fill my heart.

Like Luke, I remember when Mom made an emergency trip back to the States with Dad. I remember being very scared that Mom would die, and I would never see her again. I also remember Mom skipping our little adventure through Europe and the Middle East. Not sure if this was because of her sickness or just her being smart enough not to go on a Rapid Robert tour (which included several countries in only a couple weeks)! My guess is that she was quite sick.

Mom, I just want to say thanks, and I love you! Thanks for being there for me even when you didn't feel well. Thanks for doing such a great job raising four high-energy boys. Thanks for teaching us all how to live so gracefully despite your continued health issues.

Matt Cropsey, Second son of Bob and Shirley Cropsey

> After leaving Togo, **Matt** went to Bob Jones University and came away with an Airframe & Powerplant license along with a pilot's license. He has worked the past 20+ years as an aircraft mechanic in the Columbia, South Carolina, area. He lives with his wife, Mandy, and their three kids: Matthew, Anna, and Caroline. He continues to be involved with church and missions.

Mom was Always There for Us

Seems like Mom has been sick with something or other pretty much our whole lives; well, at least since I was five years old. I remember the headaches beginning in Canada while we were in Sherbrooke (attempting) to learn French. (One thing I have learned about the Cropsey family is that we don't do well with foreign languages to begin with!)

Seems like even through all the struggle, Mom and Dad would always love on people they met. I think it was the language tutor that came to teach Mom French in Canada because she had missed so much class whom they began a Bible study with. Even though Mom never felt "great," she always took care of us and taught us how much God loved us and cared for us. We stayed in Canada an extra year, supposedly for Mom's sake, but Dad benefited from the extra language study as well!

When we finally got to Togo, Mom was involved with teaching us. She taught us how to love people even when it wasn't convenient. She was always sharing Christ and bringing people closer to Him, challenging people in their walk with Jesus!

She was involved in getting the cuisine ministry going at the hospital. That meant, of course, that the missionary kids were responsible for doing the Bible lesson every Tuesday. Again, this was part of her master plan in training her children to know how to communicate Christ to the lost whom were all around us with many great needs.

Mom put up with our shenanigans (probably our Irish heritage). She would make us run laps around the house, or make us lunchboxes and tell us to go explore the jungle for the day. She let us grow up as "pure boys"! We had a Yamaha YZ60 that we terrorized the countryside with; we had animals that we captured or purchased that seemed to die at alarming rates; we had large groups of visitors we would host; there were kid groups we helped manage; there were "chores" that were established for us to keep up with; there was church; there was visitation; there was hospital visitation; there were special occasions; and even vacation were adventurous! Through it all, Mom somehow was always there for us!

I can honestly say that there is no mom in the world that could beat our mom! She is one of a kind, and the best in all the world!

Part One Notes:

1. The food was organized by the ladies at Calvary Baptist Church, our sending church, located in Ypsilanti, Michigan. The food included mixes, chocolate chips, nuts, pudding, jello (mostly used like Kool-Aid. It did not gel well in the heat), etc. It was a wonderful thing for these women to do. However, I had put together a labeling system, and some of the ladies decided it would be a great joke not to label them correctly! It was a disaster on my end. I only used the special items in Togo if we were having company or it was a special occasion. Opening a can thinking you were going to use a certain item, and it was something totaling different was difficult when there were no stores nearby or items readily available to buy. But, we made it through, even with this inconvenient dilemma.

A farmer who lived next to my parents had purchased a barn loft of candy bars for his pigs. He offered to give us some to take to Togo, and that is the way we had candy to can! It wasn't too bad if you didn't know or remember what the fresh stuff tasted like.

2. Poem used by permission. Story of A.M. Overton: https://www.churchlead.com/mind_wanderings/view/1630/he_maketh_no_mistake

3. A note about the possible origins of this quote and the influence it had on the American culture: https://quoteinvestigator.com/2014/05/09/urgent/

4. The ministry that started in our second semester in Canada was a ministry of correspondence. I began hearing from many different people; some gave advice

about healing solutions and others were in the midst of their own challenging health needs. We didn't share a lot about our personal struggles with everyone through our general prayer updates, but I was able to share on a deeper level how God was faithful, His plan was good, and He was sovereign! I was also able to be transparent with several I wrote to about discouragement in language learning and with my health. There was also the disappointment of not getting to go to Togo in the time we had planned, etc. I was often very encouraged by their stories.

I was also able to do some special things that I might not have done if I were in school full time. That included baby showers, taking meals to other mom students, getting to know some of our neighbors, and just being more in tune with the kids' school activities. As my energy increased, I got so I was able to keep John home with me, too, instead of sending him to the nursery at school. These were precious times. I think I appreciated them more realizing how close I'd come to some very difficult side effects of the encephalitis! Of the six encephalitis patients the doctor had in Kalamazoo, three had died, one was left blind and deaf, another at the time was bedridden and not expected to live, and the other was me! It is often a terrible disease if left untreated. I had progressed so much by Christmas that they really didn't do any kind of treatment but told me to rest and pray for God's healing.

5. My growing up years were during a time when my grandparents believed that children were to be seen and not heard! My grandma was a believer, but my very

moral and upright grandpa was not until the night my dad died in a roadside accident.

My grandpa was a changed man inside and out. He would eat ice cream sitting in the middle of the living room floor with my boys. He and Grandma took them for a hot dog roast in the middle of the cow pasture and flew kites. He would call up and see if the boys wanted to do chores with him. The behavior was so foreign from my own experience with him. My grandma and grandpa were becoming more and more aware of the true gift that their children, grandchildren, and great-grandchildren were to them.

My grandpa was also the one in the family that labeled me the "black sheep," challenging me not to take the boys to Africa and raise a bunch of "jungle bunnies!" His argument included these points: Would they be safe? How would they be educated? Didn't they need family close?

He was not a happy camper with me! John, our youngest, was two and a half years old when we left for language school. God drew my children and grandparents together through tragic circumstances and now God was going to pull them apart? God never promised that life would be easy; in fact, He told us to count on trials and tribulations.

Some verses about spiritual heritage: Exodus 20:5, Deuteronomy 6:7, Deuteronomy 12:28, Deuteronomy 4:9, Deuteronomy 11:19

Part Two Notes:

1. Romans 3:10, Romans 3:23, Romans 6:23, Romans 5:8, Romans 10:9 & 13

2. In the beginning, I had everything including our underwear ironed. I didn't want to get the bot fly egg in our skin! The bot fly laid its egg in clothes that were on the outside line to dry (which we all did). After a while in Togo, we didn't iron everything anymore. We never did have any bot fly infestations.

3. You can tell we were new missionaries at that point. I was unfamiliar with drugs and tropical diseases and infestations! Bob was making a list of drugs to pick up to have at the house for us and the many who came to our house for medical help once the word was out that Bob was a doctor and the hospital was not yet open.

4. Yes, this was 1983! There was no such thing as digital photos. We had film, and pictures needed to be developed.

5. Animist and voodoo were very present in Togo at this time.

Part Three Notes:

1. My mom had just been diagnosed with colon cancer.

2. The adult worm cannot be killed with medication and lives from 12 to 15 years. The micro filariasis, when sloughed, cause side effects that can be controlled to an extent with treatment. There were 11 different parasite pandemics when we arrived in Togo.

Acknowledgments

My husband Bob is my "gift" from the Lord. He has loved me well, encouraged me, cared for me, and continues to be my spiritual hero. He is the father of our children. Both Bob and our children have taught me so much on this earthly journey. Thank you, Lord, for my family.

I would be remiss if I didn't give God thanks for my mom! She kept the letters I wrote to her year after year, documenting God's faithfulness. My mom and dad lived life at home just as they did in public. They loved the Lord and were always showing others that "love," especially to us three kids. Thank you, Lord, for my family.

Then there are our churches, filled with fellow pilgrims on life's journey: Volinia, where I grew up; Calvary, our sending church; Kpodzi, our Togolese church; and all our supporting churches. Thank you, Lord, for keeping them faithful!

Aly, this testimony to God's faithfulness wouldn't have come to fruition if it weren't for you and the many hours of work: sorting, filing, reading, typing, and editing. Thank you, Lord, for giving Aly the gifts necessary to bring this project to life.

It is a humbling experience to lay before others my weaknesses and frailty! On the other hand, it is exhilarating to be reminded of how God has directed my life. He has remained faithful through all the challenges. To your Name be all the glory! Thank you, Lord.

Shirley Cropsey

Enjoyed this book? Check out:

- *A Surgeon's Hands - God's Work: The Life and Medical Missions Career of Dr. Bob Cropsey* by Ernie Bowman

- *One Candle to Burn* by Kay Washer with Alison Gray